WEST COAST 4-6-0s AT WORK

WEST COAST 4-6-0s AT WORK

C.P. Atkins

LONDON

IAN ALLAN LTD

Dedication
To Matthew and Stephen

First published 1981

ISBN 0 7110 1159 1

© C. P. Atkins 1981

Published by Ian Allan Ltd, Shepperton, Surrey;
and printed by Ian Allan Printing Ltd at their works
at Coombelands in Runnymede, England

Contents

Jacket painting: 'Claughton' class 4–6–0s Nos 5908 and 5981 climb Camden Bank with the down 'Mancunian', c1929. *George F. Heiron*

Title page: Caprotti 'Claughton' No 6023 seen at Crewe in July 1939. *T. G. Hepburn/Rail Archive Stephenson*

Left: Deputising for a Pacific, No 45524 *Blackpool* tackles the southbound ascent to Shap with a 15–coach Birmingham train in October 1957. *W. J. V. Anderson*

Introduction

Quite apart from numerous statistical superlatives the former London & North Western could justifiably lay claim to having been the most literate of the many pre-1923 British railway companies. Did not two of its most senior officers, respectively General Manager and Superintendent of the Line no less, record for posterity in a most lucid manner a graphic account of the Premier Line in the late 19th century? Thus we have *The Working and Management of an English Railway*, by George Findlay (1889) and *Railway Reminiscences* by George P. Neele (1904). Somewhere between the two, in 1893, appeared *British Locomotives, – their history, construction, and modern development*, by one C. J. Bowen Cooke, 'outdoor assistant, LNWR locomotive department.' Three years later an opposite number in the CME's department of the Lancashire & Yorkshire Railway, George Hughes, produced *The Construction of the Modern Locomotive*. Few could have foreseen in 1896 that a quarter of a century later Hughes would succeed Bowen Cooke as CME of the LNWR.

In 1890s both men were yet to make their mark, but having assumed supreme office on their respective lines during the next decade both were to make significant public utterances. The highlights of these have been succinctly put together by E. S. Cox

in *Speaking of Steam* (Ian Allan Ltd, 1971). Cox himself threw new light on the locomotives of Hughes and Bowen Cooke in his classic paper 'A Modern Locomotive History – Ten Years Development on the LMS – 1923 to 1932' delivered to the Institution of Locomotive Engineers in January 1946.

The melting pot of 1923 was not particularly kind to the locomotives of the former LNWR, with the notable exception of its later 0-8-0 classes. The operator of numerically some of the largest locomotive classes to have seen service in the British Isles, the LNWR locomotive fleet has not proportionately received undue attention in the literature. Its close friend and neighbour the LYR was very much a closed book in this respect until 1954 when the situation was remedied by one of its former servants, the late Eric Mason. Such a paucity of knowledge is, however, not true of the Caledonian. Its 4-6-0s in particular have received detailed attention by the writer in *The Scottish 4-6-0 Classes* (Ian Allan Ltd, 1976) and largely on this account, but also because of their relatively very small numbers, they have collectively rated only a single chapter here, which incidentally deliberately omits reference to the McIntosh 5ft 9in mixed traffic classes, and ex-Highland 'Rivers'.

In this book I have sought to concentrate on those aspects of the locomotives under review which have hitherto escaped close attention, and have hopefully succeeded in presenting some new facts. In this regard I have been aided by access to certain material which has only recently become publically available, in the Library of the National Railway Museum. This includes LMS locomotive test reports, and the registers of Crewe Locomotive Drawing Office (seven volumes covering the period 1890 to 1930). To detail the fundamental biographical particulars of each of the 680 LNWR 4-6-0s would demand an excessive amount of space and the task has recently been accomplished in Volume 2B (LNWR) of *The British Locomotive Catalogue 1825-1923* (Moorland Publishing Co, 1979).

In researching this book I am indebted to Messrs Kenneth Cantlie, E. S. Cox, G. R. M. Miller, and J. W. P. Rowledge for generous technical assistance, to Messrs G. H. F. Atkins, T. J. Edgington, and J. P. Wilson for assistance with illustrations and to my wife, Christine for cheerful help and encouragement.

C. P. Atkins,
Harrogate,
August 1980.

Below: No 5984 at Nottingham Midland, c1932. *G. H. F. Atkins*

1
The West Coast 4-6-0s

During the first two decades of the 20th century the 4-6-0 was to the West Coast main line, what the 4-4-2 was to the East Coast Route. Thus in the year 1910 one could travel the 401 miles between Euston and Glasgow behind black London & North Western and blue Caledonian Railway inside-cylinder 4-6-0s. One's corresponding 393-mile journey from Kings Cross to Edinburgh would be behind green Great Northern and North Eastern Railway outside-cylinder 4-4-2s. The 4-6-0 had actually made a comparatively fleeting appearance on front rank express passenger services on the North Eastern around 1900, but had been quickly superseded by Wilson Worsdell's larger Class V 4-4-2 in 1904. Only the Great Northern, the most extensive British employer of the 4-4-2 type, really exploited the latter's capability to accommodate a wide firebox.

Four coupled wheels, with up to 42 tons resting thereon, remained adequate for the heaviest duties on the comparatively easily graded East Coast Route until about 1920. Then, in the closing months of their independence in 1922, both the GNR and the NER moved on from the 4-4-2 to the 4-6-2, thereby presenting the London & North Eastern Railway upon its formation the following year with the prototypes of a new generation of heavy passenger power. The subsequent classic development of the Doncaster 4-6-2 has been more than adequately covered elsewhere.

The situation on the rival London, Midland & Scottish Railway in 1923 which was to compete with the LNER for the Anglo-Scottish traffic, was less than happy. Between Euston and Glasgow the 4-6-0 still held sway, but since 1910 it had been enhanced with the provision of the superheater and substantially enlarged, thereby requiring the adoption of three or four cylinders. For a brief period it was conceivably possible to travel north over the West Coast main line successively behind multi-cylindered 4-6-0s of increasing size and modernity. These each effectively represented the ultimate design philosophy of the three drawing offices of Crewe, Horwich and St Rollox, whilst these still retained their independence.

Thus in 1922 one could depart from Euston behind a LNWR 'Claughton' four-cylinder 4-6-0, which although possibly of quite recent construction dated back in design 10 years to 1912. At Crewe a rather more modern and capable looking Lancashire & Yorkshire Railway four-cylinder 4-6-0 might await, also painted black, to take the train on over the 141 arduous miles to Carlisle. The basic design of this locomotive actually dated back five years earlier still, but after 11 years the design had been completely modernised with the provision of superheater and piston valves. Its presence at Crewe, especially paired with a large eight-wheeled tender, was but one manifestation of the recent amalgamation of the LNWR and LYR, whereby although the latter lost its name it gained the upper hand in terms of overall administration.

At Carlisle, if one was fortunate, a blue Caledonian Railway three-cylinder 4-6-0 built only the previous year to an entirely new design, would be standing at the north end of Citadel station waiting to take the train on to Glasgow. Despite its majestic appearance the Caledonian engine shared two grave impediments with its two English predecessors, erratic steaming and poor coupled axlebox lubrication.

Of more simple design and construction the superheated LNWR 'George the Fifth' and Caledonian 'Dunalastair IV' 4-4-0s suffered no such inhibitions and could be thrashed mercilessly. As a consequence, in normal everyday running their sustained power output fell little short of that of the larger 4-6-0s. The total weight of a 'George' (less tender) approximated only to that resting upon the coupled wheels of a 'Claughton', and any advantage which the latter might show was probably more due to its superior adhesive qualities rather than its larger (or should one say, longer?) boiler. The spectre of Shap, whose summit stood 926ft above sea level, with its associated long ascents both northbound and southbound, could well have been responsible for the rapid proliferation of the 4-6-0 on the LNWR, which after 1919 could actually boast more passenger 4-6-0s than 4-4-0s on its stock books. In addition during 1903-1909 Crewe built 200 small-wheeled 4-6-0s, which were intermediate with the LNWR's similarly rapidly expanding fleet of eight-coupled heavy goods engines. When compared to its contemporaries Crewe appeared to favour an additional coupled axle, building 4-6-0s rather than 4-4-0s, and 0-8-0s in preference to 0-6-0s.

Thus on 31 December 1921, out of a total locomotive stock of 3,336, the largest of any contemporary British railway, the LNWR owned no fewer than 621 4-6-0s, of which almost 500 had inside-cylinders, with more still building, whilst an entire class of 30 4-6-0s had already been scrapped. This was rather more than half of all the 4-6-0s then in service in the British Isles, and the nearest contender, the Great Western, could only boast 138 4-6-0s out of its locomotive stock of 3,148.

Swindon, however, had the last laugh. In 1950 when the last LNWR 4-6-0 passed to the scrapyard the former was still building 4-6-0s directly developed from Churchward's basic designs of 45 years earlier. Also the LNWR had failed to appreciate the finer points of the design of a GWR four-cylinder 4-6-0 which briefly graced its metals in 1910, and proceeded to produce the 'Claughton', whose fate was indirectly sealed when history all but repeated itself 15 years later.

Second only to Swindon in regard to its 'scientific' approach to locomotive design was the Horwich Works of the LYR. Nevertheless Horwich's *magnum opus*, its four-cylinder 4-6-0, barely equalled Crewe's 'Claughton' and likewise improvements in detailed design came too late to save the class from an early demise, despite a theoretical life of 40 years.

Superficial appearances apart, finesse was not a notable attribute of Scottish locomotive design. On the Caledonian Railway generous bearing surfaces in the Drummond tradition meant its engines could be thrashed, which in conjunction with their rather small grate areas resulted in heavy fuel consumption.

The Caledonian had its own physical obstacle to climb, comparable with Shap, in the shape of Beattock bank whose summit stood still higher at 1,015ft above sea level. St Rollox built two large-wheeled 4-6-0s in 1903, two years before Crewe produced the 'Experiments', but despite this lead and repeated attempts to produce a satisfactory 4-6-0 over the course of nearly 20 years, nothing six-coupled which was comparable with the classic 4-4-0 'Dunalastair' breed was evolved. In 1922 only eight large-wheeled 4-6-0s were working regularly between Glasgow and Carlisle, whilst new 4-4-0s continued to be added to stock, which if necessary took a pilot on the heavier trains.

This, then, was the situation on the West Coast main line in January 1923. To their credit the first two CMEs of the LMS produced a succession of wide firebox 4-6-2 proposals during 1923-1926, which were thwarted by internal politics.

Construction of Sir Henry Fowler's four-cylinder compound Pacific had actually begun when all work on the project abruptly ceased in the early autumn of 1926 following the appearance of the brand new GWR four-cylinder 4-6-0 No 5000 *Launceston Castle* between Euston and Crewe. Spending some 5-6 weeks on the LMS this was also tested between Crewe and Carlisle, quietly and efficiently demonstrating in the process what a large well-designed 4-6-0 could be capable of. Only a week after the termination of the trials a large high pressure *three*-cylinder 4-6-0 was outlined in diagram form at Derby, and precisely one month later still on Boxing Day 1926 a firm order for 50 such engines was received in Glasgow by the North British Locomotive Company. The 'Royal Scots' handled the cream of the West Coast heavy passenger traffic for several years, establishing entirely new standards of thermodynamic and mechanical performance which completely eclipsed those of the Crewe 'Claughtons' and Horwich 'Dreadnoughts', which are the principal subjects of this book.

West Coast 4-6-0s, 1922

Right: LNWR 'Claughton' class four-cylinder 4-6-0 No 499. *Ian Allan Library*

Below: Rebuilt Hughes LYR four-cylinder 4-6-0 No 1511, with eight-wheeled tender, departs from Crewe with a down West Coast express.

Bottom: Caledonian Railway three-cylinder 4-6-0 No 958, one of two such engines stationed at Carlisle (Kingmoor), but recorded at Balornock shed in October 1922.

2
The Webb 4-6-0s

Francis William Webb was undoubtedly the most prolific of British locomotive engineers, as well as one of the most controversial. Between October 1871, when he succeeded John Ramsbottom as Chief Mechanical Engineer of the LNWR, and mid-1903 when Webb underwent an enforced retirement, Crewe Works turned out approximately 2,800 new locomotives. Of these only almost 500 were the compounds, nowadays immediately associated with Webb's name, some of which were actually completed after his departure.

To put matters still further in perspective, only 100 of these were of the notorious 2-2-2-0 and 2-2-2-2 'uncoupled' variety. These were outnumbered 4 to 1 by 80 4-4-0s, 30 4-6-0s and 281 0-8-0s whose driving wheels *were* coupled together.

Not least on account of his own formidable personality, and autocratic iron grip on affairs both domestic and mechanical at Crewe, Webb has traditionally received something of a bad press. There has been a tendency to overlook the simplicity and longevity of his earlier locomotive designs. These followed very much in the Ramsbottom tradition, with which Webb himself would have been closely associated as Chief Draughtsman and subsequently Chief Assistant to Ramsbottom during 1859-1866, prior to leaving the LNWR for five years before returning as CME in 1871. Even regarding his later period Webb scarcely appears to have been accorded the credit due as the first British builder *in quantity* of eight-coupled heavy goods (the LNWR built no 0-6-0s after 1902), and multi-cylinder locomotives, albeit compounds.

Although particularly smitten with a three-cylinder compound system which involved the provision of a single enormous low pressure cylinder between the main frames, Webb latterly came to favour *four*-cylinder compounds. He also built one of the first British four-cylinder simple locomotives for comparative purposes in 1897. This 4-4-0, which was soon converted to a compound, incorporated piston valves, (which were also applied to the high pressure cylinders of some of the later 2-2-2-2 and 0-8-0 three-cylinder compounds) then very much in their infancy, if only in a primitive solid head form. The compound version, which utilised piston valves only for the outside high pressure cylinders driven by rockers from the LP Joy valve gear between the frames, was multiplied to 40 units. Known as the 'Jubilee' class, this was not unduly large even by contemporary standards. In July 1901 a further series appeared, the 'Alfred the Great' class, in which boiler girth and heating surface were increased. Forty of these were built up to late 1903 but they were only palliatives, and hopes that they would obviate double heading were dashed. The late R. E. Charlewood, a keen commentator of contemporary LNWR locomotive affairs, did not rate the 'Alfreds' as highly as the preceding 'Jubilees' and claimed that they were very expensive in lubricants and very heavy on repairs.

The simple truth was that Webb was not able to keep pace with the rapidly increasing weight of British express trains at the turn of the century, of which the LNWR had to work some of the heaviest over one of the longest and most difficult main lines in the country. In October 1900 the LNWR General Manager, Frederick Harrison, towards whom Webb entertained a pathological dislike and refused to allow to set foot within the confines of Crewe Works, had issued his famous edict that from henceforth all express passenger trains loaded in excess of the equivalent of 17 six-wheelers were to be piloted. For these purposes eight-wheelers were regarded as $=1\frac{1}{2}$, and the sumptuous 12-wheeled diners, $=2$. This led to anomalies, because in practice $=17$ could vary from 270 to 320 tons. Coupled with the changeable and frequently adverse weather conditions in the vicinity of Shap, difficulties inevitably arose.

It was at about this time that the first of several frequent reports appeared in the press as to Webb's alleged impending retirement. This was strenuously denied by Lord Stalbridge, the LNWR Chairman, and a close friend of Webb. The latter clung to office, however, not in the arrogant belief that he was irreplaceable, but through a morbid fear of abject poverty in retirement. This, and periodic bouts of irrational behaviour were but symptoms of a mental decline associated with an unspecified hereditary illness. Webb's eventually enforced retirement took effect from the end of June 1903, and when he died in Bournemouth just three years later he left the truly enormous sum, by contemporary standards, of £211,543.

The ultimate LNWR compound locomotive design was a rakish four-cylinder mixed traffic 4-6-0, – a wheel arrangement which one does not readily associate with the name of Webb. The prototype No 1400 was officially photographed at Crewe on 7 March 1903. The earliest relevant entry in the Crewe Drawing Office Register, for a frame drawing, is dated 10 January 1903. Indeed, the frames would have been the only major piece of new design work involved as the boiler, cylinders and internal Joy motion were interchangeable with those of the Class B four-cylinder compound 0-8-0 goods engines. The leading double-radial truck, the term bogie was not strictly accurate when applied to LNWR locomotives, was similar to that of the 'Jubilee' and 'Alfred' 4-4-0s, whilst with typical Crewe thrift the coupled wheel centres with individually hand forged spokes had been salvaged from withdrawn 'DX' 0-6-0s. The tenders were of the antiquated standard Crewe wood-framed design; the Webb 4-6-0s were the last new locomotives to receive them, although whether the tenders themselves were newly built is uncertain.

Although the Webb three-cylinder compound 0-8-0s had been known as Class A, under a short-lived classification scheme adopted around 1905 the new 4-6-0s were also thus designated. A rare, and possibly unique reference to one of the latter as such, was made by the driver of No 610 in the official report following a fatal accident at Huddersfield on Good Friday (21 April) 1905 when the LNWR engine reversed tender first into an LYR train. The Webb engine was only a few weeks old and its tender bore the brunt of the damage, the accident indirectly coming about because the engine was too long for the local turntable.

More generally, the class became known as the '1400' class, after the prototype, but a popular sobriquet was to refer to them as the 'Bill Baileys' after the mythical hero of a popular song who showed some reluctance to return home. This has often been construed to indicate that the engines were notoriously unreliable on the road, but a more rational explanation is simply that the song was particularly popular at the time the class made its first appearance. Thus the GNR 0-8-0 'Long Toms' and 4-4-2 'Klondykes' reflected near contemporary events very much in the public mind, ie the South African War and Alaskan goldrush respectively.

The first Webb 4-6-0s actually displayed some reluctance to leave 'home'. The *Locomotive Magazine* for 5 December 1903 recorded that the third example had just been completed and remarked that it was a curious coincidence that each engine had so far become derailed when about to commence its trial trip! To follow the initial 10 '1400s', Webb's successor George Whale ordered a further 20 compound 4-6-0s (and actually signed the general arrangement drawing) immediately after his pilot order for five 'Precursor' 4-4-0s. Indeed the last Webb 4-6-0 was completed in March 1905, only two months before the appearance of Whale's own first 4-6-0.

Photographs of members of the '1400' class are not common, and views of them actually at work are scarce. The late W. A. Tuplin aptly described their appearance in motion as 'accidents going somewhere to happen', photographs suggest their most flattering viewpoint to have been rear three-quarter. The distinctly flat-chested appearance of the Webb 4-6-0s was, however, deceptive. As in all the preceding three- and four-cylinder compound 0-8-0 coal engines the front tubeplate was recessed some 2½ft into the boiler barrel. A horizontally hinged mesh screen, intended to function as a spark arrester, acted as a partition at the junction of the barrel and the smokebox. Any ash and char which would be obstructed by this from flying straight up the chimney, would accumulate in a cast iron hopper which protruded down beneath the front end of the boiler and between the high pressure slide bars. This fitting was later removed.

At the other end of the boiler the small shallow firebox was set well back with almost 40 per cent of its outside length overhanging the rear coupled axle. The then generous grate area of 20.6sq ft had first featured on Webb's 'Dreadnought' 2-2-2-0 of 1884, and thereafter remained standard on all his subsequent 2-2-2-0s, 2-2-2-2s and 4-4-0s, but must have imposed a severe and unnecessary limitation on sustained power output on the Webb 4-6-0s and 0-8-0s, which were otherwise quite big engines for their time.

An interesting feature of the Webb 4-6-0s, which they owed to their direct derivation from the 0-8-0s, was that suspension of the trailing coupled axle was by means of a large inverted transverse laminated spring, which passed beneath.

This was a feature of *all* the LNWR eight-coupled locomotive designs, and has incorrectly been described by the late W. A. Tuplin in *North Western Steam* (George Allen & Unwin, 1963) as having been a transverse battery of volute springs.

Our knowledge of the activities of the Webb 4-6-0s north of Crewe is almost entirely due to the contemporary writings and subsequent recollections of R. E. Charlewood in *The Railway Magazine*. Although primarily intended for service between Crewe and Carlisle, the first examples were actually stationed at Edge Hill, and it was not until the autumn of 1904 that '1400s' regularly began to work over Shap. For their benefit the maximum unpiloted limit of =17 vehicles was relaxed at the beginning of 1905 but had to be restored by the spring. It had been hoped that they would eliminate the need for double-heading altogether on the heaviest West Coast trains. Writing many years later in 1937 Charlewood amplified this by saying that the '1400s' were initially expected to be loaded up to =25 (around 450 tons) without assistance. Their performance, however, was disappointing and the highest speed Charlewood ever personally recorded behind the class was 67.3mph by No 2033 between Penrith and Carlisle. In the autumn of 1906 these 4-6-0s were again tried north of Crewe on slow and semi-fast trains without success, soon after which the new Whale '19in' 4-6-0s began to become available for these duties.

The operation of the '1400' class over Shap was thus brief, and it gravitated to the London area in 1907. It is also known to have worked between Manchester and Leeds when new, and rather later over the Central Wales line down to Swansea. During 1909-10 several '1400s' were stationed at Willesden, although not by November 1912 when 20 of them were distributed as follows:

Bletchley	1	Springs Branch	1
Nuneaton	1	Edge Hill	5
Stafford	2	Shrewsbury	1
Crewe South	2	Mold Junction	1
Bangor	2	Llandudno Junction	3
Holyhead	1		

Very few British locomotives of 20th century build were scrapped prior to the Grouping, but by 1923 the LNWR '1400' class was but a memory. One of the last built, No 321 which had emerged in January 1905, was withdrawn from service as early as October 1913, and 10 4-6-0s had been broken up by the end of 1914. Many of Webb's four-cylinder compound 4-4-0s and 0-8-0s were rebuilt by his successors, who removed the outside high pressure cylinders and reduced the bore of the inside former low pressure cylinders which then took live steam direct from the boiler. The necessary drawings to modify the surviving Webb 4-6-0s to have 18½in by 24in inside cylinders only were actually prepared at Crewe during March 1915, and then shelved. Generally speaking, during World War 1 every available locomotive was desperately required, some having been sent overseas, with others borrowed, and others lent. During 1916 and 1917 on the LNWR out of a total locomotive stock of just over 3,000, on average about 800 engines were stopped either awaiting or undergoing repair. Despite this, and their relatively recent construction, a further 16 Webb 4-6-0s were broken up before the end of 1918. The last survivor, and also the last LNWR compound built, was No 2059 of March 1905 which was withdrawn from Holyhead in September 1920.

The Webb '1400' Class 4-6-0s

Right: The second Webb 4-6-0, No 2033 stands complete but unpainted outside the Erecting Shop at Crewe in 1903. These were the only 4-6-0s on the LNWR to have their frames cut in a single piece (33ft long) owing to poor positioning of the frame slotting machines in the Heavy Machine Shops at Crewe Works. Later 4-6-0s had the first section of their underframes cut separately and spliced on.

Below: No 2033 again, in traffic in glossy lined black livery. Note the absence of knuckle joints in the coupling rods.
Rixon Bucknall Collection

Below right: No 170 prominently displays the hinged 'piano front' giving access to the rocking levers which operated the outside HP piston valves.

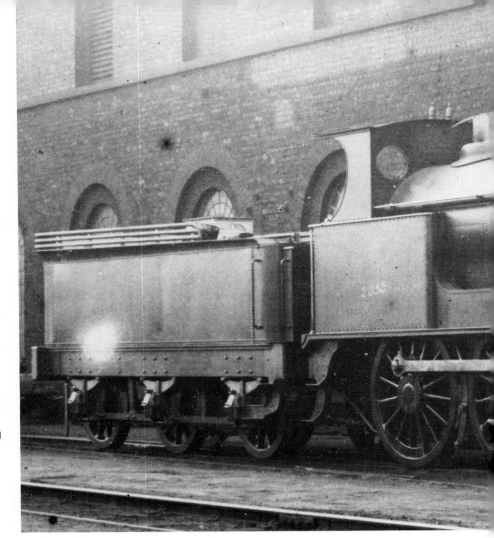

Above: The weak front end of Webb's 4-6-0 is clearly displayed by No 1729. *Rixon Bucknall Collection*

Below: No 545 in repose clearly shows that the smokebox ash-hopper has been removed, as also took place with the corresponding four-cylinder compound 0-8-0s.
Real Photographs

Webb 4-6-0s at Work

Above right: A rare photograph of a Webb 4-6-0 on passenger duties during the brief period the class was so engaged between Crewe and Carlisle. Pictured in Weston Cutting. *Rixon Bucknall Collection*

Centre right: During their short lives the Webb 4-6-0s were most consistently associated with the Chester & Holyhead line. Here an example heads a down Holyhead cattle train near Colwyn Bay. *Rixon Bucknall Collection*

Below right: With banking assistance at the rear, a Webb compound 4-6-0 climbs to Shap Summit on a freight.

3
The Whale 4-6-0s

Although Francis Webb officially retired from Crewe at the end of June 1903, his successor, George Whale had been *de facto* CME for several weeks. Whale had already actually served the LNWR longer than Webb, for no less than 45 years, having joined as an apprentice of J. E. McConnell of Wolverton when aged 16 years. Essentially a locomotive running man, Whale had held overall charge of all the running departments on the LNWR since 1899. In order to have been selected for such high posts Whale must have been possessed of considerable strength of character, and yet in reality he appears to have been a decidedly elusive personality.

The late Charles S. Lake, writing in *The Railway Magazine* immediately prior to his death in 1942, recalled his personal acquaintance with F. W. Webb, and Whale's successor C. J. Bowen Cooke, but Whale himself he had never encountered, only corresponded with. The August 1906 issue of *The Railway Magazine* was devoted to the LNWR in celebration of its Diamond Jubilee. A double page feature carried the portraits of its most senior officers, but the CME was conspicuous by his absence. In fact Whale appears never to have posed for a formal portrait by the Crewe photographer, and the only published impression of him is taken from a group photograph of 1880, which also includes a relatively young-looking Francis Webb, who was yet to build his first 2-2-2-0 compound.

Both Webb and Bowen Cooke set upon record for posterity their thoughts on certain aspects of locomotive design. Whale characteristically remained silent, but two months after his retirement through ill health in June 1909 at the age of 66, a brief review of his work appeared in *The Railway Magazine*. Unusually for those times this was written by none other than J. N. Jackson, who had been appointed Chief Draughtsman at Crewe in 1888, and was to remain thus until retiring at the beginning of 1920. Covering such a long span commencing with the latter half of the Webb era, Jackson must perforce have been something of a locomotive 'man for all seasons' in view of the very different ideas of George Whale, who would have been fully conversant with all the vagaries of the various Webb compounds. In his article Jackson tactfully observed that 'No man has done more to show what a compound locomotive can do, and also what it cannot do than Mr Webb . . . during the latter part of Mr Webb's *regime* at Crewe, the weights and speeds of passenger trains increased to such an extent that the compounds were called upon to do more, single handed, than they were able, with the result that it became necessary to put two engines to haul the main line express trains, – a practice which certainly could not be defended on economic grounds.'

Jackson's prolonged presence at the heart of locomotive design at Crewe for over 30 years must have been a major factor in the remarkable continuity in the superficial appearance of LNWR locomotives over such a long period, which was almost without parallel elsewhere except on the Great Western Railway. His lengthy tenure of office was also undoubtedly responsible for the slavish allegiance to certain technical features, of which the most notable was Crewe's long addiction to Joy valve gear, first adopted in 1880 and which continued to be put into new locomotives built there until as late as 1923. Although Jackson's initials endorsed all drawings, T. E. ('Tommy') Sackfield, Leading Draughtsman from 1892 until 1922, was generally considered to be the real *eminence grize* of latterday LNWR locomotive design.

During the late spring of 1903, with Webb still nominally in charge, Whale initiated a major modification to Webb's ultimate passenger locomotive design, the 'Alfred the Great' 4-4-0, by providing independent Joy valve gear for the outside high pressure cylinders. HP and LP cylinders could now be notched up independently, and although a final 10 engines were then still under construction, an already existing locomotive No 1952 *Benbow*, was fitted up for trial. On 27 September 1903 with 372 tons in tow it made two round trips from Crewe to Stafford and back, indicator cards being taken at the same points en route on both journeys. On the first run the original arrangement was simulated by locking the HP and LP valve gears together and notching up both simultaneously with the regulator partially open. Average speed was 40.3mph, average IHP 624 and maximum IHP 835. On the second run, the regulator was fully open with the HP and LP valve gears notched up independently. The improvement was dramatic, speed averaged 46.3mph, IHP averaged 815, and peaked at 949.

The other 'Alfreds' were all swiftly converted during the next year or so, but even by the time the trial with *Benbow* took place drawings were well advanced for a large simple-expansion inside-cylinder 4-4-0 with Joy valve gear. A lesser innovation, yet still of note, was to be a steel-framed tender in place of the crude wood-framed vehicle of basically Ramsbottom design, which accompanied all Webb's tender locomotives. The prototype, No 513 *Precursor,* emerged from Crewe Works in March 1904. At 59½ tons without tender, it was the heaviest 4-4-0 yet to be built for a British railway. Before the month was out, on Sunday the 27th, it hauled 375 tons from Crewe to Rugby and back with the little Webb 6-wheeled dynamometer car behind the tender. On the up run the IHP averaged 1,002, and on the return a maximum of 1,197 IHP was recorded at 52mph on the level, and a maximum speed of 75mph attained.

Not surprisingly the 'Precursors' revolutionised LNWR passenger services south of Crewe, where large numbers were rapidly built, sweeping away in two or three short years almost all the Webb 2-2-2-0s and 2-2-2-2s, many of whose names and numbers were taken over by the new 4-4-0s. At the beginning of the winter of 1904-5 Crewe Drawing Office turned to developing a 4-6-0 more suited to the arduous Crewe-Carlisle route. The prototype, No 66 *Experiment* made its initial trip on 8 May 1905 and only 13 days later was put to the test with 373 tons, including the Webb dynamometer car, departing from Crewe at 10am prompt for Carlisle.

Inevitably interest concentrates on performance between Carnforth and Carlisle, a 63-mile stretch which was covered at an average speed of 51mph. IHP averaged 880, with a maximum of 994 recorded at 32mph on a rising gradient of 1 in 133 mid-way between Grayrigg and Oxenholme. A maximum speed of 78mph was attained down the 1 in 125 at Clifton on the descent towards Carlisle, which was nevertheless reached 20min outside the booked 163min, and more time was lost on the return run.

Compared to the 'Precursor' 4-4-0 the 'Experiment' 4-6-0 weighed 5½ tons more and had the advantage of an extra 2½sq ft of grate area. As mechanically the two designs were very similar (except for a rather shorter connecting rod in the 4-6-0), the lower sustained and maximum power output of the larger engine was presumably due to its inferior steam generating capacity. The 'Experiment' boiler was developed directly from that of the 'Precursor', the barrel, and therefore the tube length, being increased by 7¾in and the firebox length by 10in. Of the same bore the firetubes were slightly reduced in number, although in both classes the original totals were subsequently reduced as Crewe had a tendency to overcrowd its boilers. Free gas area in the 'Experiment' was therefore lower in relation to grate area than in the 'Precursor', where it approached 20 per cent, which in conjunction with the deep grate between the coupled axles allowed the 4-4-0s to be thrashed mercilessly. On the 'Experiment', with its close-pitched slightly smaller coupled wheels the longer firebox was of necessity carried above the intermediate and trailing coupled axles, the top of the foundation ring being only 18in below the brick arch as against 32in in the 4-4-0. Being longer and shallower the grate was more difficult to fire on the 4-6-0 and demanded considerable skill, which had not necessarily been mastered after No 66 had been barely a fortnight in traffic. Ashpan design was also cramped.

The differing characteristics of the 4-4-0 and 4-6-0 boilers prompted an academic investigation, with Whale's permission and assistance, by Dr F. J. Brislee of the University of Liverpool, who presented his findings to the Institute of Mechanical Engineers in March 1908. By means of a water manometer attached to representative 'Precursors' and 'Experiments', which operated over nearly all the major LNWR routes, Brislee monitored smokebox vacua. He found these normally to lie between 5 and 6in, high by modern standards, with occasional maxima as high as 10-12in. Smokebox gas analysis, to establish the efficiency of combustion, showed the 4-6-0 to do better in this respect than the 4-4-0, on account of the thin fire essential to ensure equable steaming. On the 'Precursor' Brislee found the air supply to the thick firebed in the deep firebox to be a limiting factor. At the end of his paper he suggested that improved fuel economy might result by augmenting the air supply to the grate. Crewe Drawing Office took the matter up late in 1908 and prepared a scheme for an air blower, which was to be mounted at the leading end of the tender, belt-driven off the latter's middle axle, to be connected by a flexible duct to the ashpan. Regrettably there is no evidence that this interesting proposal was put into effect.

C. J. Bowen Cooke, apologising for Whale's absence, made an interesting contribution to the subsequent discussion. He revealed that over a five month period commencing in October 1907, the coal consumption and time keeping of 4-4-0 No 276 *Doric*, and 4-6-0 No 1987 *Glendower,* had been logged between Euston and Crewe. The 'Precursor' ran a total of 34,348 miles and consumed 882.25 tons of coal, whilst the 'Experiment' covered 34,013 miles on 793.4 tons of fuel. Coal consumption therefore averaged 57.53 and 52.25lb per mile respectively, yielding an economy of 10 per cent in favour of the 4-6-0. Assuming an average speed of 50mph corresponding firing rates per square foot of grate would have been 130 and 104lb. As regards timekeeping, the 'Precursor' on average gained 79 seconds on the schedule, compared to 69 seconds by the 'Experiment'. South of Crewe the 'Experiments' were permitted to take =20½ vehicles, as against =19½ by the 'Precursors'. Over this route the late Cecil J. Allen writing in 1909 considered that the larger coupled wheels of the 4-4-0 gave them the edge over the greater adhesive weight and slightly larger boilers of the 4-6-0s.

Later revelations by Bowen Cooke for the year 1910 indicated that the 'Precursors' averaged 69,124 miles between general repairs, as compared to 64,835 by the 'Experiments'. The ratio of these two mileages accords with the respective coupled wheel diameters. With new tyres the 4-4-0s had 6ft 9in wheels, and the 4-6-0s 6ft 3in. LNWR diagrams and correspondence, however, always quoted these dimensions with the tyres half worn, as 6ft 6in and 6ft 0in respectively. Although the official boiler working pressures for both classes was 175lb some contemporary writings suggest that in some 'Experiments' at least this was increased to 195lb possibly to make 'stronger' engines of them.

The initial order for 'Experiments' had been for five engines only, and towards the end of August 1905 these took up regular duties between Crewe and Carlisle. A few weeks later they were supplemented by 'Precursors', which had hitherto not been permitted north of Wigan. Interestingly, no discrimination was made between the two classes regarding maximum unassisted loadings over Shap. Both were given pilot assistance from Carlisle to Shap Summit for loadings of above =18. R. E. Charlewood, whose admiration for the 'Precursors' was unbounded, writing later in *The Railway Magazine* for January 1907, remarked that by comparison the best work of the 'Experiments' was poor. He went on to say 'the engines have never equalled the work they did in their earliest days', – a back handed compliment which was also to be awarded a few years later to the 'Claughtons'. He continued 'their uphill speeds are not remarkable, punctuality being attained by fast downhill speeds, though indeed a large number of the trains entrusted to them are easily timed semi-fasts which call for no special effort'. In March 1908 he was to say 'the "Experiments" have, indeed, consistently maintained their reputation for high speed downhill, though their performances uphill and on the level have at times been curiously disappointing'.

There is no doubt that the 'Experiments' *were* very fast downhill, speeds in the lower eighties were commonplace on descents from Shap Summit in both directions, especially through Tebay. Writing in *The Railway Magazine* for November 1905 Charles Rous-Martin recounted a recent run behind No 66 *Experiment* with 320 tons from Crewe to Carlisle. The final 31½ miles from Shap Summit to Carlisle were covered in 29min 41 sec easing carefully down the bank and past Eamont junction and approaching Carlisle 'the speed was sometimes very high'. It was not until writing more than a year later, in March 1907, that Rous-Marten nonchalantly remarked *en passant* that the train had attained 93mph! No higher speed was ever authentically recorded on the LNWR, and it is somewhat ironic that this should have been achieved by a 4-6-0 of indifferent reputation rather than by an outstanding 4-4-0.

During 1907 'Experiments' began to work regularly between Euston and Crewe. Pick of the bunch was No 1987 *Glendower* of Camden Shed, which regularly worked the 2pm down Corridor Diner from Euston to Crewe, where during 1909-10 Preston-based sister engine No 2116 *Greystoke* took the train on to Carlisle. At the Border City awaited the legendary Caledonian Railway 4-6-0 No 903 *Cardean*, to power the final stretch to Glasgow, – 401 miles of inside-cylinder 4-6-0 haulage. Also in 1907 'Experiments' began to appear at Holyhead, and to work down the West of England line to Shrewsbury. It was on such a duty that No 2052 *Stephenson* came to grief entering Shrewsbury at excessive speed during the early hours of 15 October 1907. The still new engine overturned killing both its crew and 16 other people, including railway servants who were in the train. This disaster was the last of three of a similar nature which had occurred during 1906-7, the others being at Grantham (GNR) and Salisbury (LSWR).

George Whale's period as CME was characterised by a persistent and serious shortage of locomotives. This first became manifest in 1904 when with indecent haste a rapid start was made in scrapping Webb's 2-2-2-0 compounds, which although not liked by their drivers actually were more popular with the firemen than Whale's coal eating replacements. The major reason, however, was an upsurge in traffic which it was (wrongly) believed could be met by producing larger rather than more locomotives. Thus total train mileage worked on the LNWR in 1907 was 50,366,364 or 8 per cent up on 1905 (46,671,624) during which time total locomotive stock actually *fell* from 3,035 to 2,973. Passenger services north of Crewe were particularly badly affected in 1908, when on at least one uncelebrated occasion the Caledonian brought successive West Coast expresses into Carlisle, where there were no LNWR engines available to work them south. Such crises precipitated the premature retirement through ill health of the Northern Division Running Superintendent, and undoubtedly underlay the otherwise rather surprising construction of a further 60 'Experiments' at Crewe during 1909-1910. This brought the total to 105, as against 130 'Precursors'.

Also to cope with the traffic boom, largely sandwiched between the two main batches of 'Experiments' were 170 rather similar engines with 5ft 2½in coupled wheels popularly known as the '19in goods'. The first of these appeared in December 1906, clearly intended to perform those duties which the Webb '1400s' had failed to fulfil. During the years 1906-1909 new locomotive construction at Crewe Works attained a consistent annual total of

90 units, and in 1908 output consisted entirely of the new mixed traffic 4-6-0s.

Contrary to popular belief the boilers of the '19in goods' were not interchangeable with those of the 'Experiments', advantage was taken of the smaller coupled wheels to provide a firebox 6in deeper. Furthermore, the steeper inclination of the cylinders and motion which *were* interchangeable, resulted in a shortening of the boiler barrel by 1½in.

The '19in goods' were very widely distributed over the LNWR system, from Carlisle down to Swansea. Examples were even stationed on the East Coast for prior to July 1915, in addition to a passenger engine (successively a 'Precursor', a 'George' and latterly a 'Prince') which worked the Hull-Liverpool services, two '19in' 4-6-0s were outshedded at Hull Dairycoates (NER) for several years. Within its limitations the class evidently gave every satisfaction, but only five months after it made its first appearance Crewe proposed an inside-cylinder 2-8-0 in April 1907. This would have incorporated the same design of boiler, cylinders, and coupled wheels. The latter would have been equally spaced at 6ft 3in centres, the second pair would have carried thin flanges, and the third pair no flanges at all. The leading and trailing coupled axles would have been allowed ¼in lateral play. Some detailed drawings were prepared, but the design was not proceeded with, which was one of the very few known LNWR unfulfilled locomotive projects.

One of the minor mysteries of latterday LNWR locomotive policy was that, despite having wholeheartedly adopted superheating in all new main line locomotives built from 1912 onwards, no attempt was made to convert its fleet of 275 saturated steam 4-6-0s built during 1905-1910, although several 'Precursors' were subsequently rebuilt with superheaters and piston valves. There were, however, two exceptions. In 1912 one of the '19in' 4-6-0s No 2607, was rebuilt with the Phoenix

Right: Sectional arrangement drawing of front end of LNWR 4-6-0 No 1361 *Prospero*.

Below: Proposed Whale inside-cylinder 2-8-0 of April 1907, designed in some detail, but incorporating several major components of the already established '19in' goods 4-6-0.

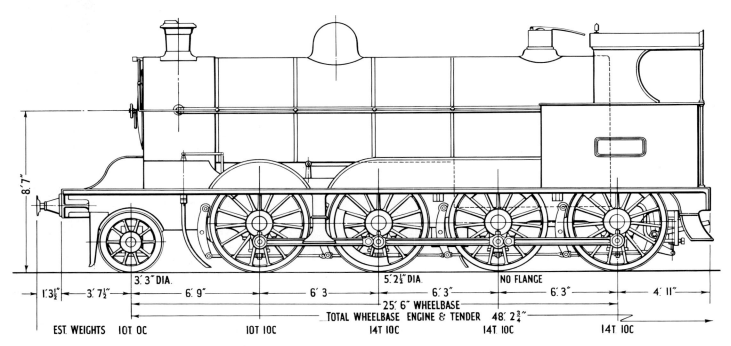

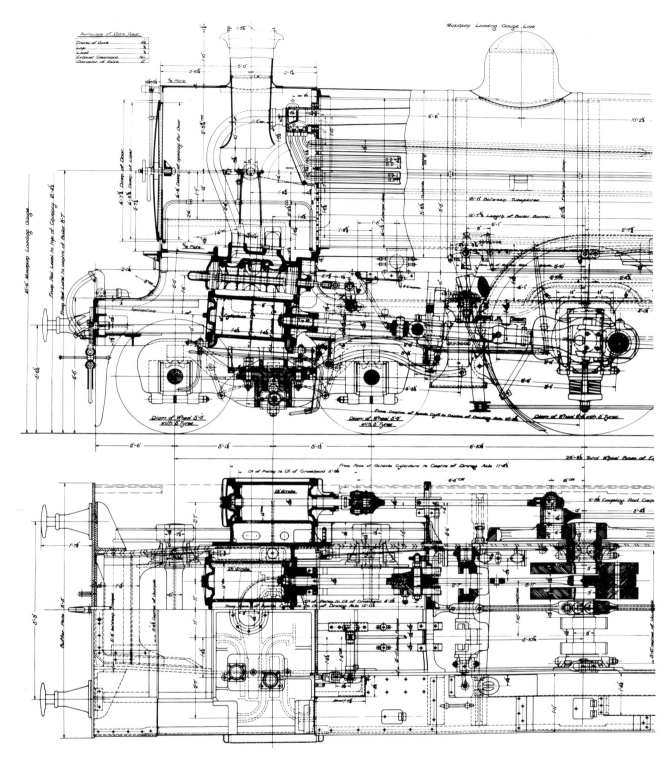

smokebox superheater. This required an extension to the smokebox upon which the chimney was perched on the leading end. Although requiring no alteration to the boiler tubes, access to the latter was rendered difficult and as with other applications elsewhere the equipment was found not to justify itself and it was removed in 1914.

During the winter of 1914-15 'Experiment' No 1361 *Prospero* was extensively rebuilt with a superheated 'Prince of Wales' boiler and four cylinders, which functioned according to Dendy Marshall's recent patent (BP 18,805/1911). Better known as a historian of early locomotives, C. F. Dendy Marshall, a Surrey

barrister who died in 1944, had devised a system for four-cylinder locomotives whereby the piston valve heads of a pair of adjacent inside and outside cylinders were mounted on a common spindle which was thus actuated by one set of valve gear. One valve head served both cylinders which had to be offset by practically their own length, but an additional non-functional head had to be included for balancing purposes. In *Prospero* cylinder diameter was 14in, and piston valve diameter no less than 12in, which must have resulted in high clearance volumes.

What induced Bowen Cooke to give trial to this system, which was not taken up anywhere else, is not known. Five months after emerging from Crewe Works in its modified form, *Prospero* worked a 393 ton test train from Crewe to Euston on 29 August 1915, when indicator diagrams were taken. These revealed a commendably equal division of labour between each end of each cylinder, but the highest IHP of which there is record was a modest 864, attained at a speed of 55¾mph on the level. When compared to 49 standard 'Princes' coal consumption per mile averaged 62.7lb as against 68.1lb, whilst the inevitably higher maintenance costs were offset by an appreciably higher mileage between heavy repairs, 58,365 as compared to 46,666. Nevertheless, *Prospero* was to remain unique, surviving in its modified form until scrapped in 1933.

Scrapping of the standard 'Experiments' by the LMS commenced in 1925, when 10 replacement Belpaire boilers (still without superheaters) were built at Crewe, one of which was fitted to *Experiment* itself. A shortage of boilers resulted in two 'Experiments' receiving superheated 'Prince' boilers during 1925-26, but these engines retained their original short smokeboxes and slide valve cylinders.

About 75 new Belpaire boilers were built for the '19in' 4-6-0s during 1925-1930. In the Belpaire replacements applied by the LMS to all three classes of ex-LNWR inside-cylinder 4-6-0s during this period, grate area was increased from 25 to 26sq ft by lengthening the firebox by 4in *forwards* and shortening the boiler barrel by a corresponding amount. This required a minimum of alteration to the frames and pipework, and in practice engines rebuilt with new pattern Belpaire boilers would sometimes revert to the original round-tapped design at the next overhaul.

Many of the '19in' 4-6-0s were also provided with a particularly cumbersome-looking form of bogie brake by the LMS, in an attempt to augment the notoriously low braking power of Crewe locomotive designs. At least one was provided c1930 with a Deuta speed recorder, although in a rare contemporary reference to a run behind one of these engines when new, a maximum speed of 66mph was recorded, which was not unduly high in relation to what the 'Experiments' could achieve.

A handful of '19in' 4-6-0s survived nationalisation in 1948 and were allocated BR numbers which were never carried. The final example, formerly LNWR No 2615 built in August 1908, subsequently LMS No 8824, and allocated BR No 48824, was withdrawn from service in February 1950 having run 879,424 miles. This was also the last of 680 LNWR 4-6-0s to remain in service.

The Shed Allocation of Whale LNWR 4-6-0s on 7 November 1912

Shed No		'Expt'	'19in'
1	Camden	1	18
2	Willesden		2
3	Bletchley	1	
4	Nuneaton		2
5	Northampton	2	
6	Bescot		1
8	Rugby	3	2
9	Walsall		1
10	Aston		6
(10)	Monument Lane		3
13	Bushbury		5
15	Crewe (North)	35	
(15)	Crewe (South)		7
16	Longsight		8
(16)	Stockport		1
17	Farnley Junction	5	14
(17)	Hull (Dairycoates)		2
19	Chester	1	
20	Huddersfield (Hillhouse)	1	10
21	Bangor	3	
22	Holyhead	1	6
23	Warrington		6
25	Wigan (Springs Branch)		4
26	Edge Hill	3	17
27	Preston	11	3
28	Oxenholme	1	
29	Carlisle*	?	?
30	Shrewsbury	2	3
31	Abergavenny		6
33	Swansea		1
34	Patricroft	4	7
	Total	74	135

* The allocations to Carlisle (Upperby) were not recorded.
NB The first column gives the LNWR shed numbers, those given in brackets indicate sub-sheds.

The Whale 'Experiments'

Below left: Pick of the 'Experiments', No 1987 *Glendower* at Euston c1907.
Rixon Bucknall Collection

This picture: 'Experiment' No 1413 *Henry Cort* heads a down West Coast express at Farrington, near Preston.
Rixon Bucknall Collection

Bottom: Showing the flag, No 1471 *Worcestershire* on the GWR at Exeter St Davids, August 1910.

Above: 'Experiment' No 1553
Faraday hauls a heavy down
West Coast Express at Shap.

Right: An unidentified
'Experiment' raises the
echoes with an up goods
south of Bletchley c1918.
Note the bogie guard plates to
protect the journals from
water picked up by a pilot
engine, a common practice on
the Midland Railway.
F. W. Goslin

Below: About three years
later (1921) to judge from the
evident drought conditions,
'Experiment' No 2643
Bacchus in plain black livery is
seen at work in south
Westmorland.

Above left: Photographs tend to suggest the sun was generally shining at Kenton before 1923! On a bright summer's day the last 'Experiment' built, No 1658 *Flintshire* heads a down semi-fast past this then still delightfully rural area.

Left: Amid rather more gloomy surroundings No 165 *City of Lichfield* pilots an unidentified 'Claughton' at Huddersfield, c1923.

Below: No 1412 *Bedfordshire* c1923, sporting Ross pop safety valves and lined black livery.

Top: During 1925–26 10 'Experiments' were rebuilt with non-superheated Belpaire boilers by the LMS. One such was No 5525 *Byzantium* which has also acquired 'Prince'-type coupled wheel centres. As a general rule all ex-LNWR inside-cylinder 4–6–0s rebuilt with Belpaire boilers also received modified cabs to conform to the Midland loading gauge. *Real Photographs*

Above: An interesting combination. 'Experiment' No 1988 *Hurricane* still in LNWR lined black livery, paired with crimson lake tender from 'Prince' No 5770.

'Experiments' in Decline

'Experiments' were still to be seen in the London area up to the early 1930s, one or two, including *Experiment* itself appearing on St Pancras–Southend services for a time, c1925. (Below), No 5472 *Richard Moon* one of two 'Experiments' rebuilt with 'Prince' superheated boilers in 1926, is pictured at Willesden in September 1932. Two years earlier No 5464 *City of Glasgow* (right) was recorded working an up parcels train at Willesden in July 1930. *E. R. Wethersett*

The Whale '19in' 4-6-0s

Above: Mixed traffic 4-6-0 No 2000 (the only LNWR engine ever to carry this running number) seen at Euston.
Rixon Bucknall Collection

Below: The '19in' 4-6-0s were directly developed from the Whale 'Experiments'. The close resemblance is here clearly shown in this stirring view of No 2609 piloting 'Experiment' No 2622 *Eunomia* out of Carlisle Citadel, on a heavy up West Coast express.

'19in' 4-6-0s at Work

Above left: The '19in' 4-6-0s could be encountered all over the LNWR system. Here one heads a mixed train near Colwyn Bay. The formation includes two Caledonian Railway six-wheeled vans.
Rixon Bucknall Collection

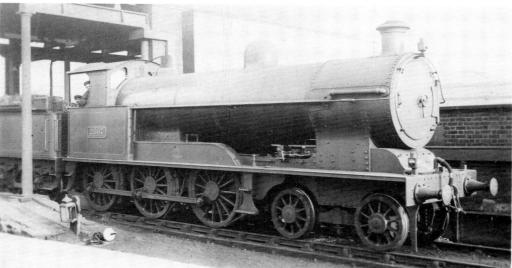

Left: '19in' 4-6-0 No 2607 disfigured by extended smokebox housing the so-called Phoenix superheater. The engine ran in this condition for only about two years before reverting to standard.

Below: Another example heads a down goods on the West Coast main line near Oxenholme.
Rixon Bucknall Collection

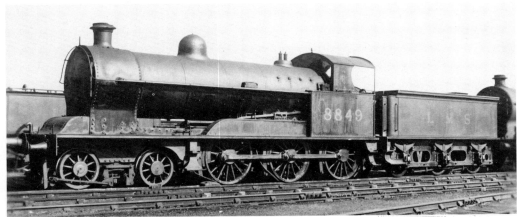

Above right: LMS No 8706 as rebuilt with Belpaire boiler.

Right: '19in' 4-6-0 No 8849 fitted with bogie brakes, and final pattern of Bowen Cooke tender. Note thin coupled wheel tyres and modified cab. *Ian Allan Library*

Below: LMS No 8834, one of three '19in' 4-6-0s which survived nationalisation in 1948, seen at Springs Branch Shed (Wigan) the final haven for the class, in September 1948, shortly prior to withdrawal. *J. P. Wilson*

Above: No 8875, unusually paired with Webb wooden framed tender, seen at Barrow on a Preston train in August 1932.

Below: No 8800, fitted with bogie brakes and Belpaire boiler, paired with Whale pattern tender at Shrewsbury.

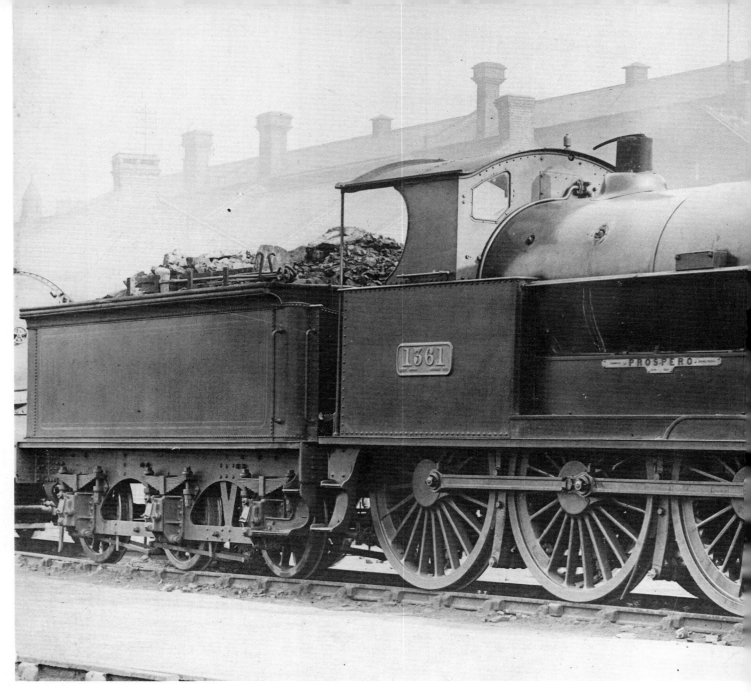

Prospero

Odd man out amongst the 105 'Experiment' 4-6-0s was No 1361 *Prospero*, which during the winter of 1914–1915 was rebuilt with a 'Prince' superheated boiler, and four cylinders. Steam distribution to the latter was effected by a novel system patented by a Surrey barrister-at-law, C. F. Dendy Marshall.

Above: Still in LNWR livery, No 1361 is seen at Camden in early LMS days.   *W. J. Reynolds*

Left: As LMS No 5554 *Prospero* heads a freight near Coventry, about 1929.   *A. Flowers*

Right: No 1361 passes through Chester, amid some typical LNWR signals, on a freight train during the World War 1 period.
Rixon Bucknall Collection

4
'Experiments' put to the Test

Whale's 'Experiment' class was the most prolific amongst the numerous British Edwardian saturated steam 4-4-2 and 4-6-0 designs. During 1909-1910, immediately prior to the widespread adoption of superheating, it ran in direct competition against its 10-wheeled counterparts on the Great Western, Caledonian and North British railways. As a result LNWR 4-6-0s worked as far north as Glasgow, and relatively as far south and west as Plymouth (which strictly speaking is more easterly than Glasgow). During this same period 'Precursor' 4-4-0s ran on interchanges between Kings Cross and Leeds with a Great Northern large-boilered 4-4-2, and a superheated LB&SCR I3 4-4-2T on special through workings between Rugby and Brighton.

In view of Whale's failing health and his succession in office by Bowen Cooke at around the time the interchanges were initiated and actually took place, it is difficult to decide who was responsible. It speaks volumes for the modesty of the Locomotive Department of the self-styled Premier Line that it should have contemplated seeing what it could learn from elsewhere. In 1908 Wolverton had completed a rather lavish bogie replacement for the little Webb Dynamometer Car. Technically this was no advancement in that likewise it could only plot drawbar pull and speed and carried no integrator nor accelerometer such as featured on the contemporary GWR and NER test vehicles. The new LNWR car became cynically regarded by the rank and file, especially in Bowen Cooke's time, as the CME's special saloon for weekend fishing trips and the like. This view was not entirely without foundation in that it was luxuriously appointed within in order to double as a director's saloon, and no particularly extensive use appears to have been made of it before 1923. Less versatile than the slightly later and much more sophisticated LYR Dynamometer Car, in LMS days it therefore was designated Dynamometer Car No 2 and was employed on more mundane locomotive tests, but nevertheless functioned quite a good deal during the 1930s. In 1946 it was converted for use in connection with some flange force measuring experiments and was not finally condemned until August 1968, after a life of just 50 years.

The Whale Dynamometer Car was only employed in those tests which were carried out at the behest of the LNWR, and where the 'Experiments' were concerned this only meant the interchange with the Caledonian. Thus on 15 June 1909 none other than CR 4-6-0 No 903 *Cardean* in all its sky blue splendour worked up to Crewe from Carlisle, to commence a 25 day sojourn south of the Border. It was reported at the time that an 'Experiment' was also working between Carlisle and Glasgow, concerning the possibility of which doubt has been expressed comparatively recently on account of the more restricted Caledonian loading gauge. Although an 'Experiment' stood some 6½in taller than was theoretically allowable on the CR, photographic evidence that No 1405 *City of Manchester* did indeed reach Glasgow Central unscathed has recently come to light, and is reproduced elsewhere in this book. No details of No 1405's exploits in Scotland have ever materialised, and it is only recently that extensive data concerning *Cardean's* performance between Crewe and Carlisle has been discovered, thereby scotching a popular myth that this had been quite exceptional.

Below: General Arrangement drawing (elevation) of LNWR 'Experiment' class 4-6-0 (1905).

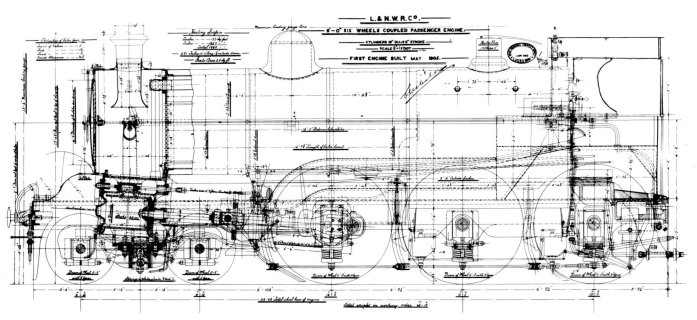

Writing in *The Railway Magazine* for November 1936 and quoting from official sources, O. S. Nock stated that on 6 July from a standing start at Penrith, with 361 tons tare/390 tons full behind the tender, Shap Summit was reached in 18½ minutes, or half a minute outside the schedule. Writing many years later in his book *The Caledonian Railway* (Ian Allan, 1962) Nock suggested that this would have entailed a sustained output for 16 minutes of the order of 1,400-1,500EDBHP. In *The Railway Magazine* for July 1956 presenting a graded league table of outstanding British steam locomotive performances, based on the magnitude and duration of drawbar horsepower per square foot of grate area, the late W. A. Tuplin rated No 903's performance south of Carlisle as the most outstanding by a non-superheated British steam locomotive.

Whilst researching *The Scottish 4-6-0 Classes* the writer considered it strange that *Cardean* should have put up such an uncharacteristically exceptional performance whilst running over a foreign stretch of line, furthermore behind schedule, and suggested a more moderate output. Early in 1977 a pair of Crewe tracings came to light at the National Railway Museum detailing the passing times, speed, and drawbar pull of No 903 and the competing LNWR 'Experiment' No 2630 *Buffalo* between Carlisle and Crewe. In both cases the dates of the southbound dynamometer car runs are one day later than those originally quoted by Nock, but far more significantly it is clear that the specified weight of train *also included the weight of the engine and tender.* Thus in reality *Cardean* was hauling only 237 tons tare, and *Buffalo* 259 tons.

Both *Cardean* and *Buffalo* were non-superheated inside-cylinder 4-6-0s of contemporary design. In both engines steam distribution was effected by slide valves located above the cylinders, actuated by Stephenson link motion in the Scottish machine, but by Joy valve gear in its English counterpart. Although boiler diameter was only slightly less in the Crewe design (5ft 2in as against 5ft 3½in) the grate was shallow and carried above the coupled axles. This would have been less suitable for an all out effort than the deeper firebox of the St Rollox product, but the latter had much longer tubes, 16ft 8in as against only 13ft, whose bore was furthermore smaller in relation to their length, so that the Crewe boiler would probably have steamed more freely under given conditions.

Considered overall *Cardean* was a rather bigger and more powerful locomotive, and its higher nominal cylinder horsepower yet lighter train loading rule out a strictly valid comparison with *Buffalo*. Between Carlisle and Preston the combined advantage in favour of the Caledonian engine on this account amounted to 31 per cent, and increased to 42 per cent south of Preston. However, it is the performance of both locomotives upon the rising gradients up to Shap Summit that are of the greatest interest, and in any case *Buffalo* appears to have had to contend with adverse signals near Lancaster and possibly beyond.

By virtue of the drawbar pulls recorded on the Crewe tracings it is possible to estimate with a fair degree of accuracy the equivalent drawbar horsepowers (EDBHP) developed. Interestingly this works out at an average of 725HP for both locomotives between Carlisle and Penrith, although *Buffalo* hauled its rather heavier load at a lower average speed. Starting away from Penrith *Cardean* developed a transitory drawbar pull of 9.9 tons, thereby slightly exceeding its nominal tractive effort (the tracing gives cylinder diameter as 19½in as against the published value of 20in). This was appreciably bettered by *Buffalo's* 11.6 tons (subsequently equalled by the Scottish engine when leaving Preston) which amounted to 122 per cent of the Crewe 4-6-0's nominal tractive effort! Between Penrith and Shap Summit, however, *Cardean's* extra beef came to the fore, the engine putting out an average 925EDBHP as against 815EDBHP by *Buffalo*.

On the final stages of the climb *Cardean* passed Shap at 52mph, at which speed it also gained Shap Summit itself, although speed actually fell to 49mph between these two points. Battling against greater odds *Buffalo* passed Shap at 45½mph falling to 43½mph before passing Shap Summit at 47mph. The 'Experiment' made a more spirited descent down the 1 in 75 attaining a maximum speed of 75½mph, despite its smaller coupled wheels (6ft 3in as against 6ft 6in), *Cardean* having touched 73½mph at the same spot. Although *Buffalo* was 75sec 'behind' *Cardean* at Tebay, the disadvantage was reversed by the time Carnforth was reached. The two locomotives both reached Lancaster in 56min 30sec from Penrith, after which *Buffalo* suffered from adverse signals losing 5min 3sec to *Cardean* by Preston, but still was only 1min 45sec outside the schedule.

The disparity in the loadings was further enhanced at Preston, and whereas *Cardean* completed the Carlisle-Crewe run in 3min 15sec inside the scheduled 166min, *Buffalo* ultimately aggregated 8min 15sec outside the time allowed.

LNWR 4-6-0 No 2630 v CR 4-6-0 No 903 between Carlisle and Preston, July 1909

	Distance miles		*Schedule*		*LNWR No 2630 259 tons 10 July 1909*			*CR No 903 237 tons 7 July 1909*		
							mph			*mph*
Carlisle	0.0	0.0	12.58	0	12.58	0.00		12.58	0.00	
Wreay	4.75	4.75			1.06¾	8.45	42	1.06	8.00	45
Southwaite	7.25	7.25			1.10	12.00	47½	1.09¼	11.15	51
Calthwaite	10.75	10.75			1.14	16.00	47½	1.13	15.00	51
Plumpton	13.0	13.0			1.17	19.00	54	1.15¾	17.45	56½
Penrith										
arr	17.9	17.9	1.22	24	1.22¾	24.45		1.21½	23.30	
dep		0.0	1.27	0	1.27¼	0.00		1.28	0.00	
Clifton	22.0	4.1			1.34	6.45	46	1.34½	6.30	48½
Shap	29.5	11.6			1.44½	17.15	45½	1.44	16.00	52
Shap Summit	31.5	13.6			1.47	19.45	47	1.46½	18.30	52
Tebay	37.0	19.1			1.52¼	25.00	68	1.51¾	23.75	57
Carnforth	62.75	44.85			2.16½	49.15	63	2.18½	50.30	65
Lancaster	69.0	51.1			2.23¾	56.30	29	2.25	56.30	56
Preston										
arr	90.0	72.1	2.49	82	2.51	83.45		2.46¼	78.15	

Another tracing exists, this time of St Rollox origin, which records the performance of both engines northbound between Crewe and Carlise. Here comparisons are not strictly valid, because *Buffalo* was more heavily loaded, and exceeding the =17 limited was given banking assistance at Tebay, unlike *Cardean* which did not warrant it.

LNWR 4-6-0 No 2630 v CR 4-6-0 No 903 between Preston and Carlisle, July 1909

	Distance miles	*LNWR No 2630 321¼ tons 9 July 1909*			*CR No 903 301 tons 6 July 1909*		
				mph			*mph*
Preston	0.0	10.55	0.00		10.56	0.00	
Garstang	9.5	11.08	15.00	62	11.08¼	12.15	63
Lancaster	21.0	11.19	24.00	65	11.19¼	23.15	64
Carnforth	27.3	11.25	30.0	63	11.25¼	29.15	63
Milnthorpe	34.6	11.32¼	37.15	58	11.32¾	36.45	59
Oxenholme	40.1	11.39½	44.30	40	11.39¾	43.45	37
Tebay	53.2	11.59*	64.0		11.58½	62.30	63
Shap Summit	58.7	12.11	76.0	33	12.08	72.0	31
Shap	60.7	12.13¾	78.45	56½	12.10½	74.30	60
Clifton	68.0	12.10¼	85.15	66½	12.17½	81.30	65
Penrith	72.3	12.14½	89.30	54	12.21½	85.30	56½
Plumpton	77.0	12.19½	94.30	62	12.26	90.0	65½
Calthwaite	79.3	12.31½	96.30	65	12.28	92.0	71
Southwaite	82.7	12.34½	99.30	73	12.31	95.0	73
Wreay	85.2	12.37	102.0	56	12.33	97.0	67.5
Carlisle	90.1	12.43	108.0		12,40	104.0	

* Banking assistance provided at Tebay.

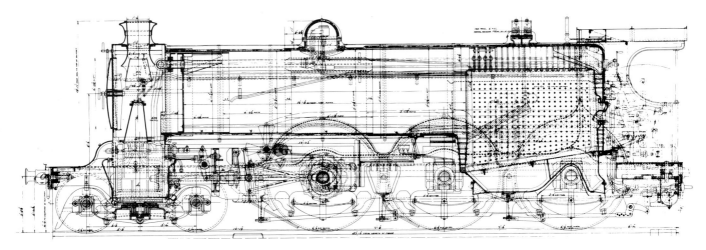

Above: General Arrangement drawing (elevation) of CR '903' class 4-6-0 (1906).

From the foregoing it will be seen that the performance of neither locomotive was exceptional, merely what could be expected of a typical Edwardian wet steam 4-6-0. At this time results very much above the contemporary norm were being achieved by one G. J. Churchward at Swindon. The Great Western directors, however, it has been claimed, were concerned at the high initial cost of Churchward's locomotives and drew unfavourable comparisons in this respect with the thrift practised at Crewe. No building costs for LNWR locomotives ever seem to have been published, but the Engine History Card for the last '19in' 4-6-0 to remain in service, originally built in August 1908, gives its original cost as £3,123. This gives a pretty good idea of the price of an 'Experiment' (the rather bigger CR '903' engines were costed at £3,500 each), and it is known that the non-superheated GWR four-cylinder 'Star' 4-6-0s averaged £3,200 apiece. On this basis it is not unreasonable to presume that the superheated 'Stars' actually cost substantially less than the later LNWR four-cylinder 'Claughtons'!

If the Great Western directors did not know when they were well off, the only instance of a GWR four-cylinder 4-6-0 running on other than its own metals before 1923 was lost on the LNWR, with whom a locomotive exchange was arranged in August 1910. The attitude of the North Western was half-hearted in the extreme, and Camden Shed sent an 8 month old 'Experiment', No 1471 *Worcestershire,* which was 45,000 miles out of shops and which could most readily be spared at the height of the summer holiday season. The trials on the GWR extended from 15 to 27 August, and a fairly detailed account of them is to be found in Chapter 5 of O. S. Nock's *The LNWR Precursor Family,* (David & Charles, 1966). It is clear that the LNW engine crew had an unenviable task, in that the water troughs on the unfamiliar GWR main line were more widely spaced and the 'Experiment' tender capacity was only 3,000gal as against the 3,500gal of the standard Churchward locomotives. *Worcestershire* was put on several of the major express turns out of Paddington, but only on one occasion was Churchward's dynamometer car attached. This was on 24 August when No 1471 hauled the 11.50am to Exeter, which was booked to cover the 173⅝ miles non-stop in just three hours, a start to stop average of 57.8mph. The initial load was 415 tons, which was successively reduced to 385 tons after Westbury, and 270 tons after Taunton, by the release of slip coaches. On the later stages of the run speeds of 75-80mph were attained, but Exeter was reached 13½min late.

For their part the GWR sent 4-6-0 No 4005 *Polar Star* to the LNWR. By this time several 'Stars' were fitted with superheaters, but to make for a fairer comparison with the 'Experiment' a non-superheated 'Star' had been selected. This worked entirely between Euston and Crewe, venturing no further north, and no consideration appears to have been given to putting the LNWR's own dynamometer car behind it, nor even to make a close examination of the GWR engine's excellent design features. This was very much a missed opportunity, but a second chance was to arise 16 years later and the outcome was to be very different. Meanwhile, back at Swindon Churchward had presumably made his point, whilst *The Great Western Railway Magazine* for November 1910, which carried an extensively illustrated feature of the exchange duly observed that 'it is inexpedient to give any figures showing the results obtained'.

No such data concerning the relative fuel and water consumptions has since emerged from either side, but almost a quarter of a century later some utterances were made to this effect concerning the one day trial of a North British Railway 4-4-2 and a LNWR 'Experiment' 4-6-0 between Preston and Carlisle on 24 October 1910. In his Presidential Address to the Institute of Transport in 1933, William Whitelaw harked back 23 years to when he had been Chairman of the NBR, which had been uncertain as to whether to order additional express locomotives to the existing 4-4-2 pattern, or to re-design these as 4-6-0s. Doubtless to have arranged an exchange trial with the rival Caledonian '903' class 4-6-0 would have been quite unthinkable and contact was made with the LNWR. *This* time there was no question of the 'Experiment' working north of Carlisle, and so an NBR 4-4-2, No 881 *Borderer,* came south. With 284 tons in tow the Scottish engine made the up journey at an average speed of 48mph, touching a maximum of 71mph, returning at an average of 52.2mph, and attaining a maximum speed of 76mph. The competing 'Experiment' was No 1483 *Red Gauntlet,* possibly chosen on account of its name having the Scott associations beloved of the NBR directorate. With the same load *Red Gauntlet* made the up run at an average speed of 48.6mph, with a maximum of 72mph, returning north at an average speed of 52.2mph and touching a maximum of 80mph. In this respect there was not a great deal to choose between the two engines, but there was a wide disparity in fuel consumption. *Red Gauntlet* returned an average of 58lb per mile, as against no less than 71lb by *Borderer.* To be fair, however, the NB crew had had little or no opportunity to familiarise themselves with the road, and by all accounts the Scottish driver was far from noted for his finesse. In the event the NBR opted for more 4-4-2s. No photographs appear to exist of this event, which was *not* the first time an Atlantic had worked over Shap, for on 4 May 1905, the pioneer LYR 4-4-2 No 1400 had worked through from Manchester to Carlisle on a race special.

The GWR and NBR trials with the LNWR during the latter half of 1910 may be regarded as the 'final fling' of the saturated steam express passenger locomotive in the British Isles. The appearance of 'foreign' 4-4-2s and 4-6-0s between Euston and Carlisle during 1909-1910 was to make no impact on subsequent LNWR locomotive practice. What *was* to have dramatic repercussions was the performance of the medium sized superheated brown tank engine from Brighton, whose appearance north of Willesden on the 'Sunny South Special' probably attracted comparatively little attention in November 1909. Savings in fuel and water consumption of more than 30 per cent would not be ignored, however, and a new era was dawning.

The LNWR v CR Locomotive Exchanges, 1909

Above: The legendary Caledonian Railway 4-6-0 No 903 *Cardean* at speed on the West Coast main line *south* of Carlisle on 23 July 1909. Behind the tender is the newly completed Whale Dynamometer Car.
Courtesy, National Railway Museum, York

Above right: Photographic evidence that an LNWR 'Experiment' *did* reach Glasgow in 1909. No 1405 *City of Manchester*, complete with CR-style route indicator heads an up West Coast express out of Glasgow Central. Nevertheless no details of this engine's performance north of the Border have yet come to light.
Courtesy, National Railway Museum, York

Centre right and below right: A fine study of the LNWR protagonist on the LNWR itself during LNWR v GWR locomotive exchanges of 1910. Nevertheless No 1455 *Hertfordshire* looks almost archaic when compared to its contemporary, GWR No 4005 *Polar Star* photographed at almost the same spot.
Courtesy, National Railway Museum, York

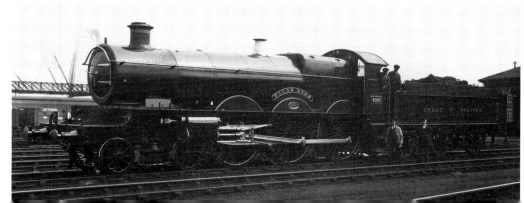

5
The 'Princes'

Following the experimental LNWR/LB&SCR Rugby-Brighton locomotive through workings Crewe Drawing Office almost immediately set to work to design a superheated version of the 'Precursors'. The result was by common consent one of the most outstanding pre-1914 British steam locomotive designs. LNWR No 2663 *George the Fifth* was outshopped simultaneously with its non-superheated consort No 2664 *Queen Mary* only eight months later in July 1910. The former was in essence a 'Precursor' with enlarged piston valve cylinders, extended smokebox and Schmidt superheater. On 24 July it hauled 357½ tons, including the Whale Dynamometer Car, from Euston to Crewe at an average speed of 60.5mph. Average IHP was 1,094, peaking at 1,229 at a speed of 64mph on the level, as against corresponding IHP values of 1,002 and 1,174 by *Precursor* back in March 1904.

In his enthusiasm to get these impressive results in support of superheating into print, in *The Railway Engineer* for November 1910, Bowen Cooke neglected to quote corresponding data for No 2664 *Queen Mary*. Concerning the performance of this locomotive very few details have come down to us, other than Bowen Cooke's own assertion that No 2663 showed a fuel economy of 26.7 per cent at 45.7lb per mile. Nevertheless a further nine non-superheated 'Queen Marys' initially were built, although the superheated 'George' won the day and the former were soon rebuilt to conform. A total of 90 'Georges' were built up to mid-1915, and many 'Precursors' were later rebuilt with superheaters, and in most such cases, with piston valves also.

Quite apart from the presence of the superheater, part of the success of the 'Georges' was due to their excellent cylinder design with direct steam ports, and relatively long travel piston valves. The early 'Georges' were given 1¼in lap and 5½in maximum valve travel, but this appears to have been fairly soon amended in later builds to 1 1/16in and 5in respectively, as in the 'Precursors'. The Joy valve gear on the 'Georges' was indeed very similar to that on the 'Precursors' except that a very short vertical rocking lever had to be interposed in order to 'invert' the motion from outside to inside admission appropriate to piston valves.

It was only to be expected that in view of the great benefits accruing from the adoption of high degree superheating that a superheated development of the 'Experiment' 4-6-0 should be put in hand. A major event to occur on LNWR territory in the summer of 1911 was the investiture of the Prince of Wales at Caernarvon Castle. The name *Prince of Wales* had so far been borne by three LNWR locomotives, including currently by Whale 'Experiment' No 1676. The latter's name plate was physically transplanted for use on the prototype of the new class, to which it gave its name, the inscribed building date being noticeably amended.

The new LNWR superheater 4-6-0s attracted very little attention, nor was the prototype, No 819, subjected to any dynamometer car tests as were accorded its illustrious immediate antecedents. Such involving the 'Princes' were not to occur until early LMS days during 1923-1925, when a maximum DBHP of 970 was recorded at a speed of 40mph. In their heyday the 'Georges' could *sustain* 1,000DBHP for 30 minutes at speeds over the 50-60mph range.

The 'Georges' undoubtedly had the edge on the 'Princes' as to performance, and some surprise has been expressed as to why the latter was preferentially multiplied to no fewer than 245 units by mid-1922. One reason would undoubtedly have been World War 1 when express passenger trains became both heavier and slower, factors which would have favoured the 4-6-0. During World War 1 'Princes' were regularly hauling 500 tons out of Euston unaided. In addition, although ostensibly an express passenger locomotive, the 'Prince' made an admirable mixed traffic machine thereby filling a notable gap in the LNWR locomotive ranks to which the Whale '19in' 4-6-0s could not aspire. Furthermore its lower axleload of 18½ tons, compared to the 19¾ tons of the 'Georges', would have conferred on the 'Prince' a wider route availability.

The outbreak of World War 1 put an immediate strain on the considerable resources of Crewe Works, which was therefore obliged to subcontract the construction of some new locomotives, which had hitherto been all but unknown on the LNWR. In May 1915 an order went to the North British Locomotive Co in Glasgow for 20 'Princes' (without tenders). Nevertheless Crewe furnished NBL with the frame plates and most of the castings and forgings, virtually leaving the contractor to build the boilers and erect the engines. To preserve Crewe 'face' the LNWR style number and nameplates proclaimed the engines had been built at Crewe. This rather conflicted with the NBL builder's plates on the smokebox sides which professed origin to have been the latter's Hyde Park or Queens Park Works between which construction was divided for speed of delivery. In these engines the steam brake was substituted for the vacuum brake, and the balance weights in the driving wheels were graceful cast steel crescents, in place of the rather clumsy pattern of the 'Experiments' and early 'Princes'. The NBL-built 'Princes', delivered during the winter of 1915-16 were also the last LNWR passenger locomotives to be turned out new in the fully lined black livery. During 1915-16 Crewe also had on hand 30 'Princes', to which it added 65 more during 1919-1920.

Although the latter were turned out plain black, following an LNWR Board decision of October 1921 to restore the old livery, a few examples of this batch were running fully lined out by 1923. Amongst them was No 1351, which had been so repainted at Horwich Works in August 1921 following overhaul there preparatory to some experimental, and evidently not particularly distinguished running on the LYR involving the use of the latter's dynamometer car.

Early in 1920 orders were placed with William Beardmore & Co of Dalmuir, Glasgow for no fewer than 90 'Princes', and 60 tenders.* During and immediately after World War 1 another

---

*This contract was worth £900,000, and probably constituted the largest single order for locomotives to be placed with a private builder by a British railway prior to 1923.

armaments giant, Vickers, had repaired LNWR '19in', 'Experiment' and 'Prince' 4-6-0s at its Openshaw (Manchester) and Barrow establishments.

When completed the Beardmore 'Princes' were normally coupled in pairs cab to cab and towed 'dead' over Beattock minus chimneys and dome covers. Their motion was erected at Crewe, and finished in a dull leaden grey paint the engines ran trials, some with their numbers chalked on the cabsides. Their numberplates were to have been cast and affixed at Crewe, but an internal industrial dispute there delayed this being carried out.

With the arrival of the last 'Prince' from Beardmore's in April 1922 the class mustered 245 units, and for so large a class was remarkable for its apparent homogeneity. Superficial variations were practically confined to sand boxes, balance weights, style of tender framing and presence or absence of superheater dampers. There was, however, not inconsiderable 'invisible' variation as to valve gear and valve setting.

In the early 'Princes' built up to 1915 the Joy valve gear was directly adapted from that on the 'Experiments'. In June 1915 the exhaust clearance was increased from ¹⁄₁₆in to no less than ¼in, a value actually exceeded by the long travel (5½in) 'Georges' where it amounted to no less than ⁵⁄₁₆in compared to only ¹⁄₁₆in in their 'short travel' (5in) counterparts. The short vertical rocking levers on the 'Princes' and 'Georges' experienced appreciable angularity when in full gear, having an amplitude of up to 60 degrees. This caused considerable wear in the associated pins and in order to reduce this the valve gear was slightly re-designed in June 1918, and applied to the 65 'Princes' built at Crewe thereafter in which the piston tail rods were also suppressed.

In practice the modified gear wrought no improvement and one of Bowen Cooke's last acts as CME, before going on sick leave from which he would not return, was to instigate the design of direct Joy motion in April 1920. Such had been applied to the 4-6-2 tanks from new, but on these the smaller diameter boilers and coupled wheels provided more room for such an arrangement. In order to accommodate this on the 4-6-0s maximum valve travel in full gear had to be reduced from 5⅛in to 4⁹⁄₁₆in. The new layout was experimentally tried out on 'Prince' No 429, which despite displaying a markedly uneven exhaust beat, was subsequently specified for the Beardmore 'Princes'.

A number of existing 'Princes' were also converted, but drivers did not rate the 'direct' motion 4-6-0s so highly, nor was the

avowed intention of reducing associated maintenance costs evidently achieved. During the year 1922 the average *total* repair cost of 130 'direct' 'Princes' exceeded that of the 'indirect' balance by some 17 per cent. A similar excess was chalked up by 32 similarly modified 'G1' 0-8-0s compared to their peers. In the case of the 4-6-0s this was particularly surprising as 90 of their number were of recent construction, average age only 13 months as against approximately 6 years for the remainder, as at 31 December 1922. Paradoxically the 60 'G2' 0-8-0s built new with direct motion during 1921-1922 at Crewe, mean age 10 months, averaged a mere £12 per engine, although probably the cost of fabricating the new motion for the conversions was included in the repair costs. Rebuilding with direct motion also required the substitution of new screw reversers provided with left hand threads. Joy valve gear imposed considerable stress on the reversers, which although provided with a standard rachet locking device, from about 1920 on many superheated 4-6-0s and 0-8-0s these were supplemented by a steam operated clutch mechanism.

Total repair costs direct v indirect Joy motion, 1922

Prince 4-6-0	No in class	Average repair cost per engine
direct	130	£536
indirect	115	£457
0-8-0		
G1 direct	32	£811
G1 indirect	203	£695
G2 direct	60	£12

The fact that Crewe was still persevering with Joy valve gear as late as 1920 was in itself something of an indictment. After 1900 only the LNWR and LYR persisted in fitting it to new locomotives and when these two railways formally merged on 1 January 1922, out of a combined locomotive stock of almost 5,000, around 3,000 engines were so fitted. Back in 1909 George Hughes of the LYR had proclaimed the virtues of Joy motion to be its lightness,

Below: Modified indirect Joy valve motion as applied to the 65 Crewe-built 'Princes' of 1919-20. No reduction in pin wear was effected, in addition to which as before the bolts securing the rocking lever bracket to the slide bars gradually worked loose.

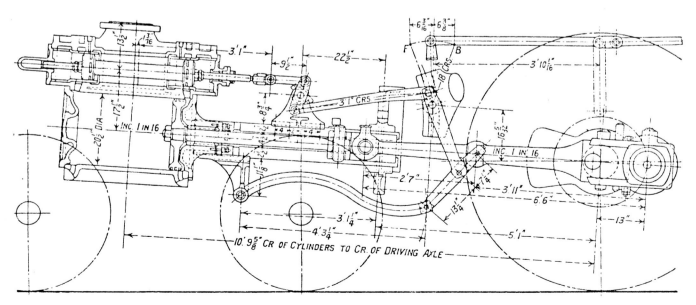

simplicity and reliability. Up to that time it had been called upon to distribute saturated steam via slide valves to cylinders of only moderate diameter, a function to which it was well suited. In the superheated LNWR 'Princes' in particular with their 20½in bore cylinders and 8in piston valves, the limitations of Joy valve gear became acute.

Whilst Joy gear eliminated the need for eccentrics it was necessary to drill the connecting rod at a particularly vulnerable point in order to take the jack link pin. It had not been unknown on both the LNWR and LYR for connecting rods to break as a direct result occasionally, although on Horwich engines the jack link pin tended to fracture first. However, during 1922 there were no fewer than seven such fractures on the 'Greater LNWR', fortunately without serious consequences.

Two of these failures occurred only seven days apart, involving 'Prince' No 877 at Cheadle Hulme on 28 April, and a 4-6-2T at Furness Vale on 5 May. Just a year later, on 28 May 1923 a connecting rod broke on a piloted 'Prince' No 1355 when it was hauling a 439ton down express at 65-70mph at Betley Road, near Crewe. In all these three failures the flailing remnant of the connecting rod still attached to the crankpin pierced the boiler barrel and/or the firebox, mercifully without causing serious harm to the engine crews.

In view of their chronological proximity the Cheadle and Furness Vale incidents were unusually dealt with by the one Ministry of Transport report. The Inspecting Officer harked back to this when commenting a year later on the Betley Road fracture, and had the newly established National Physical Laboratory perform tests on the remains of the broken rod. He further remarked on the seeming unsuitability of Joy valve gear for heavy express duties, pointing out that the design of the connecting rods of the 'Princes' was almost identical with that of the non-superheated 'Experiments' which performed much less onerous duties. Analysis suggested that fractures in the vicinity of the jack link-pin hole were triggered at speeds of 60mph and above by the interaction of complex inertia forces, coupled with high cylinder compression, notably when steam was shut off, when cylinder lubrication was also impaired.

It was suggested that Crewe should examine possible alternatives to Joy valve gear, acknowledging that such developments were indeed already in hand. Bowen Cooke's successor as CME, Captain H. P. M. Beames, had already conceived of a scheme by the end of October 1922 whereby Walschaerts valve gear outside the frames would work the piston valves inside the frames by means of rocking levers. The simple substitution of Stephenson valve gear was precluded by the presence of the sacred centre bearing on the driving axle, which had actually gradually been discarded by Horwich from about 1910. Although always referred to as Walschaerts valve gear at Crewe, Beames was granted a British Patent (No 214,065) for his new arrangement in April 1924, and for good measure also patented a new pattern of compression release valve, which was experimentally fitted to three Claughtons.

The so-called Beames valve gear was first applied to 'Prince' No 964 Bret Harte in March 1923, which ran for a while with an indicator shelter attached. On 22 April it made a test run to Carlisle and back with a train aggregating exactly 400 tons, including the Whale Dynamometer Car, and the results were given in considerable detail in The Railway Gazette only three weeks later in its issue for 18 May 1923. No IHP values were given, but running was evidently brisk, on the return run in particular, with Shap Summit being reached in 48min 45sec and Preston 109min after the departure from Carlisle, compared with 57min 30sec and 123min respectively by Experiment with a slightly lighter loading back in May 1905.

In addition to a Walschaerts conversion simultaneous with that of Bret Harte, only two other 'Princes' were so treated, this time a year later in April 1924. This pair received a modified version of the valve gear, but no more conversions were carried out because it was found that stronger connecting rods incorporated a marine-type big end introduced from mid-1923 had proved to provide a successful and cheaper alternative.

In practice it proved almost impossible to set the valves correctly on the Walschaerts 'Princes', which was probably a contributory factor to their undistinguished performance. In appearance too they were decidedly unattractive, and were popularly referred to as 'Tishies', after a contemporary racehorse named Tishy which reputedly crossed its front legs when running and thereupon fell over. Legend has it that a pair of nameplates so inscribed were actually 'struck' at Crewe in ignorance of the origin of the name, but not used. In 1932 all five 'Tishies' were reported to be in store at Shrewsbury shed, two of which were amongst the first 'Princes' to be scrapped the following year.

The fifth 'Tishy' had been completed by Beardmores' in March 1924 to form the centrepiece of their stand at the British Empire Exhibition at Wembley in that year. Finished in Derby crimson lake livery and bearing the number 5845 on the tender, at some stage during the course of the exhibition the engine received the nameplates Prince of Wales. These had been specially made, although late in 1924 ex-LNWR No 819 was reported to be running temporarily minus its nameplates, following an overhaul and repaint (to red livery) at Derby Works as LMS No 5600. No 5845 was taken into LMS stock in November 1924, and officially photographed at Crewe two months later with its nameplates in situ, although whether it actually ran in traffic with them is not clear. To complicate the issue still further another 'Tishy', No 2340 Tara, was for some reason officially photographed at Rugby in April 1924 also bearing the same nameplates, but retaining its own running number.

When built No 5845 was also unique amongst the 'Princes' in that it was fitted with a Belpaire firebox. Although a feature of the Bowen Cooke 4-6-2Ts and the 'Claughtons' prior to 1923, such was not LNWR standard practice and it seems likely that the subsequent dominant influences of Derby and Horwich caused Crewe Drawing Office to design Belpaire versions of the boilers of the principal LNWR locomotive classes late in 1923. It was just at this time that Beardmore's had approached the LMS with a view to building a 'Prince' for exhibition purposes. Copies of the new boiler drawings were forwarded to Dalmuir, and about 50 of these boilers were built by contractors c1925. Many of these were originally fitted to 'Princes' which initially retained their LNWR plain black livery and numberplates, amongst them the pioneer 'Tishy' No 984 Bret Harte. At subsequent shoppings a round-topped boiler might be restored, and indeed No 5845 (actually carrying its post-1934 number No 25845) ran with the earlier pattern for a period. One 'Prince' exchanged a round topped for a Belpaire boiler as late as 1946.

It was the 'Princes' rather than the 'Georges' which were chosen to represent Crewe in comparative trials during 1923-1925. Just why has never been made clear, but the 4-6-0s outnumbered the 4-4-0s at almost 3 to 1, and also seemed to display greater economy in their favour. By purely statistical chance the average age of the 'Princes' and the 'Claughtons' was precisely the same, but the average repair costs in 1922 of the inside-cylinder engines was just about half of that of the big four-cylinder 4-6-0s, which in turn corresponded closely with that of the admittedly rather older and hard-worked 'Georges' (see Appendix 2). LMS fuel consumption statistics for the period

1927-1936 also showed that on a lb/mile basis the 'Prince' was the lightest of the three at 51.6lb, followed by the 'Claughton', 53.0lb, with the 'George' returning 55.8lb. By 1936 however, half of the 'Princes' and all the original 'Claughtons' had been withdrawn, whilst most of the 'Georges' were still in service!

In December 1923 'Prince' No 388, with its original modified indirect Joy motion, made some test runs between Leeds and Carlisle. Although six months of out of shops, in terms of drawbar thermal efficiency it came very close to equalling that sacred yardstick of the pre-Stanier LMS, the Derby compound 4-4-0. The two designs returned respectively 4.6 and 4.45lb/DBHP hr. Eighteen months later NLB-built 'Prince' No 90 *Kestrel*, since rebuilt with direct motion and newly out of shops, when running over its home ground between Preston and Carlisle curiously showed up less well. The disparity widened in the Compound's favour, the latter returning 4.25lb/DBHP hr as against just over 5lb by the 4-6-0. Interestingly also, whereas No 388 had developed a maximum of 970 DBHP No 90 attained only 875. It would be interesting it know to what extent the two patterns of valve gear influenced the results, although this particular characteristic of the two engines does not appear to have been referred to in either report.

By 1925 the 'Princes' would have been rapidly passing their peak. A practical reason for Crewe's predilection for Joy valve gear was that it permitted the provision of a centre bearing between the webs on the crank axle. Soon after 1922 in the mistaken pursuit of increased economy the centre bearing was swiftly removed thereby putting greater strain on the main journals, with the result that 'Georges' and 'Princes' could no longer be thrashed with such impunity as hitherto. The mainframes of both were light (1in thick) and were virtually the same as those of the unsuperheated 'Precursors' and 'Experiments'. Later 'Princes' when built incorporated ¼in patchplates around the driving horns, which were in some instances subsequently applied to the intermediate horns also. Such paltry measures had little effect and in early LMS days the 'Princes' were plagued with badly cracked frames, the flaws generally commencing in the vicinity of the left hand driving horns, whilst the incidence of overheated axleboxes in that position was also high.

At this time the 'Princes' constituted a numerically strong class of comparatively recent construction whose actual rapid demise a few years later would not have been contemplated, not least on account of the economic climate. There was plenty of scope for improvement and so they came under close scrutiny early in 1931 to see what might be done.

The investigation was carried out by E. S. Cox, who 15 years later was to make public for the first time the modernised 'Prince' which was proposed as a direct result. The existing Belpaire boiler was to be raised 3in in order to permit mechanical lubrication of the axleboxes, and its pressure increased to 200lb enabling cylinder diameter to be reduced to 19½in. Austerity was to be the keynote with a high footplate carried above the coupled wheels, a side window cab and standard Fowler 3,500gal tender.

The most interesting feature of this proposal was that it was to incorporate Caprotti poppet valve gear, with a single propeller shaft located between frames actuating valves above the cylinders, after the layout applied to 10 'Claughtons' in 1928. Quite independently the inventor of the system, Arturo Caprotti himself had somewhat pre-empted the scheme during 1930 by producing detailed drawings in Milan for new 20½in by 26in poppet valve cylinders having the steam chests *outside* the frames for the 'Princes'. Beames clearly proposed to 'renew' the latter on the lines indicated above, mainly for the benefit of the accountant (as with several of the 'Claughtons') for very little of the original engines would have remained. If it be thought a new inside cylinder 4-6-0 design was an anachronism in 1931, let it be recalled that only the following year Gresley on the LNER produced the most successful exponents of this type by applying larger boilers and long travel valve gear to the ex-Great Eastern Holden 4-6-0s of LNER Class B12. New locomotive designs with inside cylinders were either built or proposed by each of the four British main line railways as late as the 1940s, and in 1942 the Belgians projected for future construction an advanced inside-cylinder mixed traffic 4-6-0 with wide firebox.

Writing in the SLS Journal for February 1978, E. A. Langridge who was much concerned with locomotive design on the LMS at that time, claimed that upon detailed investigation the use of

Below: Diagram of Beames' proposed 'Modernised Prince of Wales' 4–6–0 with Caprotti valve gear, 1931.

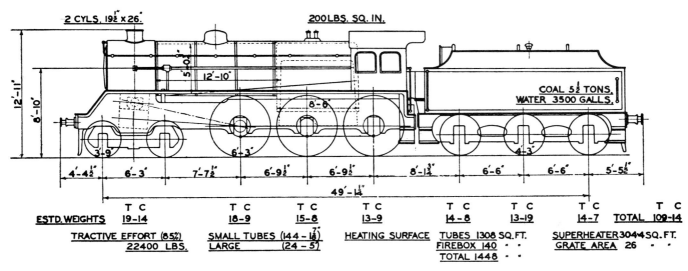

MODERNISED 4 – 6 – 0 PRINCE OF WALES DESIGN – 1931.

Valve Characteristics of LNWR 'Prince' class 4-6-0 (Piston Valves 8in diameter)

	'Expt'/'19in'	Original	June 1915	June 1918	April 1920	Jan 1923	Jan 1932	Nov 1923
Valve gear type	Direct Joy*	Indirect Joy	Indirect Joy	Modified indirect Joy	Direct Joy	Direct Joy	Indirect Joy	Walschaerts /Beames
Lap	1 1/16in	1 1/16in	i 1/16in	1 1/16in	1 1/16in	1in	1 1/4in	3 1/32in
Lead	3/16in	1/8in	3/16in	3/16in	3/16in	1/4in	1/8in	9/32in
Exhaust clearance	nil	1/16in	1/4in	1/4in	1/4in	1/4in	1/16in	1/4
Maximum valve travel in full gear	5in	5 1/8in	5 1/8in	5 1/8in	4 9/16in	4 5/8in	5 3/8in	4 3/4in

* slide valves

poppet valve gear proved impracticable on the 'Princes' within the constraints of available space and weight. He further stated that it was then proposed to revamp the design with *outside* cylinders and long travel Walschaerts valve gear. Such then, presumably constituted the 10 'Improved Prince of Wales' 4-6-0s put on the 1932 LMS locomotive building programme, which were quickly cancelled by Stanier, although the standard boilers and tenders would appear to have been made and utilised.

The concept of an outside-cylinder mixed traffic 4-6-0 thus was already in embryo at the time Stanier took over as CME on 1 January 1932, and it is interesting to note that during the design stage his Class 5 4-6-0 was referred to as the 'Rebuilt Prince of Wales' class.

Built in large numbers, the Stanier Class 5 permitted the rapid withdrawal of the 'Princes' from 1933. It had originally been proposed to eliminate them by 1938, but a handful still survived a decade later, reprieved by the approach and reality of World War 2. Bletchley and Stafford were their final strongholds, but the end finally came early in 1949.

The LNWR 'Princes'

Below: No 446 *Pegasus*, one of the 20 NBL-built 'Princes' of 1915-1916. Note circular Hyde Park Works builders plate on smokebox, soon removed. In stating that the engine had been built in Glasgow this conflicted with the number and nameplates, which claimed origin to have been Crewe!
Rixon Bucknall Collection

Top right: An early Crewe-built 'Prince' No 1400 *Felicia Hemans*. The running number is taken from the prototype Webb Compound 4-6-0, which was broken up the same month that this engine was built, January 1914.

Right: No 241, nameless like all the 90 'Princes' built by Wm Beardmore & Co of Glasgow during 1921-1922. Built new with direct Joy valve motion and lacking superheater dampers.

Below right: No 1351, one of the 65 Crewe-built 'Princes' of 1919-1920 with modified indirect Joy valve motion. Originally painted plain black, it is here seen at Agecroft Shed (LYR) in full LNWR lined livery soon after being overhauled at Horwich Works in mid-1921.

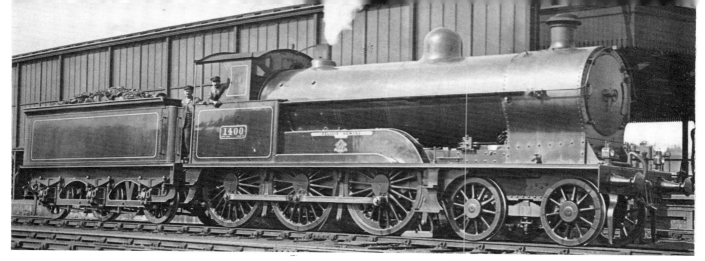

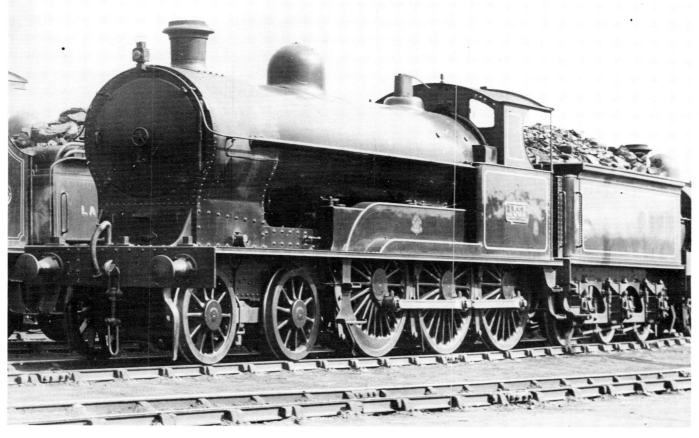

'Princes' at Work

Left: No 979 *W. M. Thackeray* when new in early 1914, on a heavy down express, which includes several 12-wheelers, near Kenton.
Rixon Bucknall Collection

Centre left: A few years later near the same location, the Watford lines having since been electrified, No 1089 *Sydney Smith*, shows signs of overwork around the front end whilst Euston-bound.
LPC

Below left: A postwar 'Prince' and train hurries over Dillicar troughs, seemingly not partaking of refreshment.
Real Photographs

Right: The Irish Mail departs from Holyhead behind 'Prince' No 2359 *Hermoine* in June 1919. Although 'Claughtons' on occasion crossed the Menai Strait before 1923, engine and tender had to be parted for turning at Holyhead, where in LNWR days 'Princes' were the largest express passenger locomotives to be stationed.
L. J. Thompson

Below: No 819 *Prince of Wales* itself, seen at Manchester, London Road.

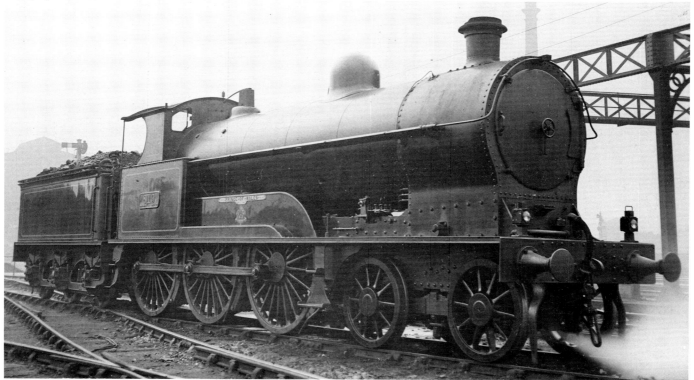

Left: 'Prince' No 522, later named *Stentor* heads a heavy up North Wales express near Colwyn Bay.
Rixon Bucknall Collection

Below left: Totally devoid of running number, No 849 *Arethusa* fitted for oil burning in 1926, at Crewe.

Bottom left: 'Prince' No 2285 departs from Colwyn Bay.
Rixon Bucknall Collection

Right: Resplendent in LMS red with number on its ROD-type tender, 'Prince' No 5714 enters Crewe from the north as viewed from the famous Spider Bridge, which appears in the background of several illustrations in this book.
Real Photographs

Below right: Also looking very smart in Derby crimson lake is No 5662 *Anzac*, which has been rebuilt with a new Belpaire boiler, and a cab modified to conform to the Midland Division loading gauge. *Real Photographs*

Above: With characteristic thrift the former LNWR had owned more locomotives than tenders to go with them. The latter frequently changed partners, and it being early LMS practice to paint the engine number on the tender, one such was provided with removable numeral panels. It is here seen behind 'Prince' No 5788, although when it later passed on to other partners this tender always remained numbered 5788. Here 'Prince' No 5788 is seen passing over Bushey Troughs. *Real Photographs*

Left: Consecutively numbered 'Princes', No 5684 *Arabic* and No 5685 *Persia* double-head the 'R101 Funeral Special', comprised of no fewer than 17 vehicles, between Euston and Cardington, at Kenton, on 11 October 1930.
Real Photographs

Below left: No 5678 *Milton* at Willesden in July 1931.
E. R. Wethersett

Top right: The prototype 'Tishy' *Bret Harte* fitted with indicator shelter, at Crewe.

Centre right: LNWR locomotive chimneys were fabricated from steel plate surmounted by a standard cast annular cap. In 1943 a fully cast replacement was designed at Crewe for application to surviving LNW tender locomotives, by then mainly 0-8-0s. The odd remaining 'George' and 'Prince' were also recipients, including 4-6-0 No 25694 seen at Crewe after condemnation in December 1947. *L. W. Perkins*

Right: No 5809 passes beneath the ancient bulwarks of Conway Castle as it is about to rumble through Robert Stephenson's tubular bridge.

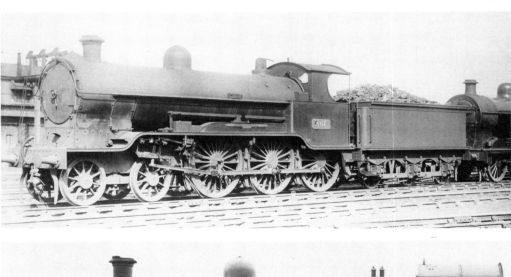

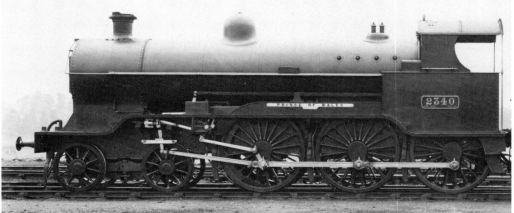

Above: Before and after, 'Tishy' 'Prince' No 867 *Condor* pilots an unidentified 'Prince' of a later series c1923.

Left: No 867 *Condor*, originally built by NBL in 1916, was one of the two 'Princes' rebuilt with the so-called Beames valve gear at Crewe early in 1923.
Ian Allan Library

Below left: A clear view of the slightly modified version of the Beames valve gear applied to two further 'Princes' early in 1924. No 2340 normally carried the name *Tara*, but for photographic purposes temporarily acquired the name *Prince of Wales*.
Courtesy, National Railway Museum, York

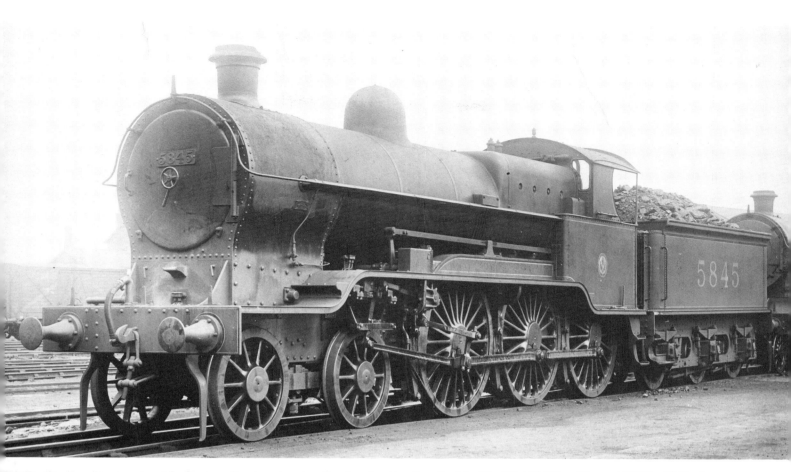

Above: LMS No 5845, the last locomotive of LNWR design to be built. Completed by William Beardmore & Co of Glasgow for display at the British Empire Exhibition at Wembley in 1924, the engine was subsequently purchased by the LMSR for £7,295. The engine bore the name *Prince of Wales* during the latter period of the exhibition. It is seen here c1925 nameless but still in red livery.
Ian Allan Library

Left: After withdrawal of *Condor* (latterly nameless) at the end of 1936 the only remaining 'Tishy' was No 5845, renumbered to 25845 in 1934, which lasted until November 1947. Much begrimed, it is here seen passing Camden on a Euston-Bletchley train in July 1939. Circa 1934–1937 this engine ran fitted with a round-topped boiler. *J. P. Wilson*

6
The Premier Locomotives of the Premier Line

A general outcome of the various interchange trials of the previous three years was the decision by Bowen Cooke in the early half of 1911 to build a large superheated four-cylinder 4-6-0. This was to owe little to the 'foreign' competitors and more to LNWR traditional practice. It was unduly long in gestation by normal Crewe standards, the Drawing Office did not tackle the job in earnest until after the first 'Princes' had begun to appear during the autumn of 1911, and it was not until 24 January 1913 that the prototype emerged from the erecting shop.

Distinctively numbered 2222, and initially un-named, within a few days the engine made a trial trip on a passenger train to Manchester. On 9 February a run was made to Rugby with the Dynamometer Car, the load aggregating 430 tons which was conveyed at an average speed of 55½mph. By the end of the month No 2222 had been adorned with the name of the current LNWR Chairman, Sir Gilbert Claughton, who thereby gave his name to the ensuing class, and who on 7 March with Bowen Cooke led the LNWR Locomotive Committee on a tour of inspection. On this occasion the engine was fitted with an indicator shelter at the front end, and the Crewe photographer was on hand.

No 2222 was shedded at Crewe North and worked a diagram which alternatively took it up to Euston and down to Carlisle, thereby covering a total of 2,008 miles per week. During May-June 1913 mileage run totalled 15,843½ miles.

Whilst unmistakably of Crewe parentage No 2222 presented a highly distinctive appearance. Preceding British four-cylinder simple 4-6-0s on the LSWR, GWR and LYR all employed divided cylinder drive, but Bowen Cooke opted for unified drive on the leading coupled axle. This followed the precedent set by Webb in his 4-4-0 and 4-6-0 compounds, but also reflected contemporary Continental practice where four-cylinder 4-6-0s on this pattern were already to be found in Belgium, Holland and Germany. Indeed in 1911 the LNWR's German counterpart, the Prussian State Railway had produced a new superheated four-cylinder simple 4-6-0 (Class S10) which remarkably anticipated the 'Claughtons' in that outside Walschaerts valve gear was used which drove the outside valves directly, and those inside through rocking levers in front of the cylinders. Whereas in the German engine driving wheels and valve gear were shamelessly exposed surmounted by a high footplate, Crewe concealed a great deal behind a deep all embracing splasher which was extended forward to envelope the steam chests. This was suitably perforated by several rectangular openings in order to enhance access for oiling purposes.

It is said that Bowen Cooke had been particularly impressed by the recent Bavarian four-cylinder compound 4-6-0s which likewise employed unified cylinder drive, and that he would have been tempted to have tried his hand likewise at a compound 4-6-0. Against him stood the LNWR loading gauge, restrictive in width if not in height. Equally potent would have been the human factor.

Barely a decade since the demise of Francis Webb it was scarcely to be expected that the men who would have to operate the engines would regard further new compounds with anything but a decidedly jaundiced eye. A near contemporary reference states that the 'Claughtons' with four *simple* cylinders were regarded as 'fancy' by the men when first introduced.

Of undeniably majestic mien, the 'Claughtons' somehow lacked the purposeful virility of the preceding Whale and Bowen Cooke inside-cylinder 4-4-0s and 4-6-0s. This was simply due to the fact that the diameter of the boiler barrel was precisely the same at 5ft 2in. Nevertheless firegrate area was commendably generous at 30½sq ft, but to match such a grate boiler diameter should have been about 5ft 6in.* In fact the Belpaire firebox was given commensurate outside dimensions but the boiler barrel itself was overcrowded, tube and flue density being some 20 per cent greater than that of the rebuilt 'Royal Scot' taper boiler, which may be regarded as the ultimate British narrow firebox locomotive boiler design.

No positive details for the original 1911 'Claughton' scheme now appear to survive, but by all accounts this would have carried a boiler of increased girth and would have been fitted with Joy valve gear. On investigation, the latter did not prove feasible whilst the newly appointed Chief Engineer, E. C. Trench, objected to the estimated weight in deference to some old London & Birmingham Railway arches beneath the main line at Camden. The scaled down boiler was therefore adopted although it has been claimed that reluctance to sanction expenditure on new flanging blocks was also to blame. These were in fact still necessary for the fabrication of the large firebox.

It was very soon believed at Crewe that the 'Claughtons' were either under-boilered or over-cylindered, for amongst the first 20 engines in place of the original 16in cylinder diameter, several were given 15¾in or 15½in bore. The 15¾in dimension was subsequently adopted as standard although this only effected a mere 3 per cent reduction in volume.

It was an engine with 16in cylinders, No 1159 *Ralph Brocklebank*, which featured in a pair of outstanding dynamometer car runs at the beginning of November 1913. On the 2nd with 455 tons behind the tender, it ran the 158.1 miles from Euston to Crewe at an average speed of 59.7mph, developing an average IHP of 1,358. Two days later, with 360 tons, the 141.1 miles from Crewe to Carlisle were covered at an average speed of 59.4mph, average IHP being 1,387. Despite a signal slack at Grayrigg, when speed fell to 15mph, Shap Summit was breasted at 37mph. The run makes an interesting comparison with that by No 66 *Experiment* only eight years earlier.

*A good rule of thumb for a narrow firebox boiler is outside boiler diameter (at firebox end) in feet = $\sqrt{1.08} \times$ grate area.

Test runs Carnforth – Shap Summit (31.4 miles, average gradient 1 in 187)

Locomotive	No 66	No 1159
Date	21 May 1905	4 Nov 1913
Train weight	373½ tons	360 tons
Time	52½min	40¼min
Average speed	35.9mph	46.8mph
Average IHP	880 (10)	1537 (8)
Max IHP	994	1669

The maximum IHP of 1,669 was determined at a speed of 69mph when ascending the 1 in 146 just below Tebay. This was the greatest power output then so far recorded by a British steam locomotive, and in terms of IHP developed per square foot of grate accorded very closely with the corresponding maximum value attained by No 2263 *George the Fifth* between Euston and Crewe in July 1910. However, in respect to *average* output on this basis over the latter run, the 4-4-0 exceeded the effort of the big 4-6-0 by just 10 per cent, with 48.9 as against 44.5 IHP/sq ft. In normal day to day running there was little to choose between the 'Claughtons' and the 'Georges', and despite their much lower adhesive weight the latter were permitted to haul only 20 tons less (ie 420 tons) south of Crewe.* Bowen Cooke and his staff were fully aware that the 'Claughtons' could be better, despite having handed out considerable data on No 1159's exploits to the technical press.

Curiously no details of fuel and water consumption were given, nor have survived, assuming that they were ever recorded. Again taking No 2663's July 1910 run as a yardstick it is reasonable to compute that north of Crewe No 1159 was consuming coal at a rate of at least 60lb to the mile at a speed of nigh on 60mph for a duration of more than two hours.

The 'Claughtons' were described fairly extensively in the technical press during the years 1913-1919. The most informative account, accompanied by sectional drawings and photographs of

*Following the advent of the 'Claughtons' in 1913, the old train loading system based on the equivalent number of vehicles was superseded by simple tonnages. It was now stipulated that no train between Euston and Crewe should exceed 440 tons, a rule which quickly lapsed during World War I.

the engines under construction, plus a resumé of the November 1913 tests, appeared in *The Railway Gazette* for 6 July 1917.

By the end of 1914 only 20 'Claughtons' were at work and the grave international situation was scarcely conducive to major development. A further 40 engines were turned out during 1916-1917 one of which, No 968, was provided with a Robinson in place of the standard Schmidt superheater. Associated with the latter were the tiresome mechanical dampers in the smokebox, which were removed from December 1918 onwards. These had served one useful purpose, however. The steaming of the 'Claughtons' was often erratic, largely due to the firetubes becoming choked with ash. The remedy was to fully close the superheater damper, the blast thereupon concentrated on the tubes sucked them clear and boiler pressure promptly rose.

Perhaps not totally unconnected with the impending demise of the superheater dampers was a modified tubing proposal of October 1918. In place of the 149 (originally 159) 1⅞in firetubes, it was proposed to substitute 105 tubes of 2¼in OD. Tube length on the 'Claughtons' was 14ft 10½in, the standard 1⅞in tubes giving an A/S ration of 1/435, compared to the later to be established optimum of 1/400. The proposed 2¼in tubes would have given a value of 1/360, or virtually the same as on the 'Precursors' and 'Georges', which also employed the 1⅞in tubes, and which hardly suffered from steaming ailments!

Earlier, in March 1916, an experimental blastpipe had been designed with what Crewe termed 'wings', but which nowadays we would call exhaust splitters. There is no record that any 'Claughton' was actually so fitted. Rather later, in 1920, there was a proposal to revive a Webb patent of 1896 whereby the smokebox would be divided by a horizontal plate, each half being

Below: Arrangement drawing of the single thermic syphon fitted inside firebox of LNWR 'Claughton' No 42 in early 1921. This experiment was only made public almost exactly 20 years later when the LNER and Southern Railway made rival claims to have introduced the thermic syphon to British locomotive practice. Note that the continuous slope of the grate on the 1920-1921 'Claughtons' was achieved simply by modifying the firebars and their bearers, the firebox itself remained unchanged.
Crown Copyright, National Railway Museum, York

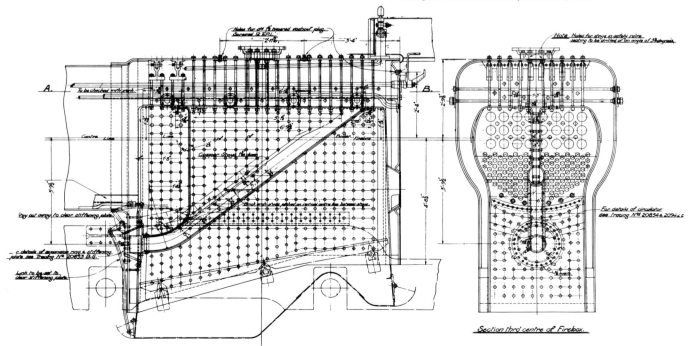

served by its own blastpipe and chimney, an idea briefly tried by Webb on two 4-4-0s and a 2-4-0. Yet another scheme mooted was to fit an oblong blastpipe and chimney. This was allegedly inspired by a recent experiment in the USA, but in fact the Crewe Drawing Office Register records a drawing for a rectangular blastpipe for the 'Experiment' class back in October 1913.

At the other end of the boiler one intriguing experiment which *was* put into effect, but not made public until 20 years later, was the provision of a single thermic syphon on 'Claughton' No 42 in 1921. Termed a 'water circulator' the arrangement drawing was signed for Bowen Cooke by Hewitt Beames, on the very day of the former's death in Cornwall, 18 October 1920. The boiler in question was successively carried by at least five different engines prior to condemnation in June 1926. Inappropriately for the fitting of a thermic syphon the inner firebox would almost certainly have been of copper, but in April 1918 a steel firebox boiler had been designed for the 'Claughtons' at a time when copper was acutely scarce, but probably not put into production.

Another advanced feature ahead of its time proposed for 'Claughtons' was an early 1923 scheme for electric lighting. At the same time drawings for a drop grate were also prepared. Two years earlier, in 1921, Crewe had also given thought to building a standard 3,000gal tender which was to run on SKF roller bearings. It is even more surprising to discover that back in 1912 Crewe had designed a roller bearing big end assembly for the 'Experiment' 4-6-0s. Contrary to external appearances, Crewe was in some respects more adventurous than Swindon!

In January 1920 delivery commenced of a further 70 'Claughtons', the last appearing in June 1921, which month witnessed the passing of Sir Gilbert Claughton himself. Despite Bowen Cooke's avowed intention to 'take the "Claughtons" in hand' once the war had ended, so urgently were the new engines required that the modifications they incorporated were minimal. These were improved cylinder lubrication, and a redesigned grate with a continuous slope from front to back. Ironically the only GWR feature incorporated in the original Claughtons was the firegrate which had a horizontal rear section behind the trailing coupled axle. It was found that the fire had a tendency to burn thin at the point where the inclination changed, which was further not assisted by the accumulation of ash upon the hump in the ashpan. Forty of the boilers for the postwar batch were contracted out to Vickers of Barrow-in-Furness, of which a feature was the employment of Ross 'pop' safety valves, which had originally been proposed for the class back in 1914.

What more fundamental remedies Bowen Cooke had had in mind for the 'Claughtons' may never be known, but in view of the loading gauge limitations on outside cylinder diameter an increase in boiler pressure cannot be ruled out. Bowen Cooke discussed the matter with Churchward but was sceptical at the latter's claim that a boiler pressure of 225lb (compared with the LNWR standard of 175lb) brought no attendant increases in maintenance costs.

When construction of the postwar 'Claughtons' commenced, it was resolved that the first should be designated as a mobile war-memorial to the former LNWR employees who had fallen in the recent war. Kenneth Cantlie was given the task of supervising its construction and at an advanced stage was horrified to discover that numberplates bearing the number 69 had been cast for it. *Soixante neuf* was a popular euphemism for brothels in Western Front parlance, and he has never been sure to this day whether or not the choice of number had been made in deliberate bad taste. (This number was subsequently allocated to the second engine of the series.) The more appropriate running number 1914 (requiring the renumbering of a 'Jubilee') was selected to go with the name *Patriot*. The engine appeared in January 1920 outshopped in the plain black livery, accorded all the 'Claughtons' when new except the initial 20. It was also suggested that a second 'Claughton' be named *Victory* and numbered 1918, but nothing came of this. No 2059 was named after its designer, whose standing was such that he rated an entry in *Who's Who*, wherein he gave his recreations as golfing, yachting and campanology. Although always known as Bowen Cooke, he in fact invariably signed drawings as 'C. J. B. Cooke'. Ultimately only 59 of the 130 'Claughtons' actually carried names, although these had been drawn up for the entire class, some as late as 1923. Three were given the names of LNWR men who had been awarded the Victoria Cross, the only railwaymen so decorated during World War 1.

At the end of 1919 the 60 'Claughtons' then in service were distributed as follows, Camden 6, Rugby 11, Crewe (North) 31, Edge Hill 7, Carlisle (Upperby) 5. During 1920 two were allocated to Longsight (Manchester), and by 1922 solitary examples were stationed at Wigan (Springs Branch) and Farnley Junction. The turntable at the latter shed was too small to accommodate it, and so the engine was obliged to run down to Leeds in order to turn on the NER table there. A similar turntable at Holyhead precluded allocation of 'Claughtons' there until early LMS days. Initially 'Claughtons' were not to be seen on the Chester & Holyhead line, partly because of their long wheelbase, but members of the postwar batch got as far as Llandudno when running in, and by the long hot summer of 1921 a pair were stationed at Bangor.

In addition to a 'Precursor', No 2222 itself was fitted up for oil firing on the Scarab system in 1920. During World War 1 the price of coal had steadily risen, and after it had ended had rapidly increased. In 1913 the LNWR had paid an average of 57p per ton for locomotive coal. By 1918 this had all but doubled to £1.05 and in 1920 stood at £1.80. In 1922 the unit cost had fallen back to £1.17. These figures graphically illustrate why several British railways were experimenting with oil firing during 1920 (when coal was scarce and being imported) *before* the Miners' Strike of the following year. A few years later, during the Coal Strike of 1926, 37 'Claughtons' and 43 'Princes' were temporarily fitted up with the Scarab apparatus.

In early LMS days it was soon established that LNWR locomotives in general were endowed with a deplorable lack of braking capacity, and many 'Claughtons' were improved in this respect from 1926. A few years earlier Crewe had evidently felt no such qualms because during the winter of 1921-22 No 2401 had participated in some brake trials, which involved hauling 300 ton trains including the Whale Dynamometer Car, between Crewe and Stafford on Sundays. No determination of the 'Claughton's' performance was made during the last days of the LNWR, other than with No 192 on the LYR between Manchester Victoria and Blackpool Talbot Road with 394 and 474ton test trains during October 1921, in comparison with Hughes rebuilt LYR 4-6-0 No 1521. It was almost as if there was a desire not to tarnish the much lauded exploits of No 1159 back in November 1913, by superseding this with data more representative of a now much more numerous class whose shortcomings were only too familiar. However, the lack of road testing of the 'Claughtons' by the LNWR was soon to be more than compensated for in the years which immediately followed 1922.

The 'Claughtons'

Top left: Two months old and fitted with an indicator shelter, No 2222 *Sir Gilbert Claughton,* with its namesake at the regulator is inspected by the LNWR Locomotive Committee on 7 March 1913. Also accompanied by G. R. Jebb, Bowen Cooke gazes affably down on four more directors. All present would in due course have 'Claughtons' named after them.
Courtesy, National Railway Museum, York

Centre left: A 'Claughton' in its prime. The third 'Claughton' built, No 1191 *Sir Frank Ree* at Crewe North in August 1913. Epitomising the elegance of the design as originally conceived, only the first 20 built were turned out new in the traditional LNWR lined black livery. The lower corners of the buffer beam were soon clipped to improve clearances, and the superheater dampers discarded after 1918.
Courtesy, National Railway Museum, York

Left: Weight restrictions in the vicinity of Camden inhibited the design of the 'Claughton' boiler, with the result that performance was variable. No 2239 *Frederick Baynes* of 1914, since repainted in wartime unlined black livery tackles Camden bank with a miscellany of LNWR stock.
Rixon Bucknall Collection

Below: Un-named 'Claughton' No 85 passes over Bushey troughs with a down express soon after the grouping.

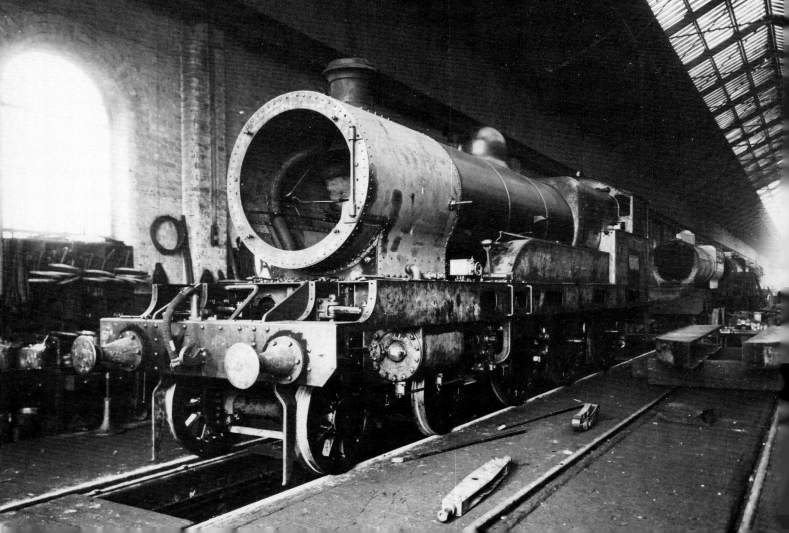

'Claughtons' Under Construction

Left: A 'Claughton' on the stocks at Crewe in 1917. Note the large 24-element Schmidt superheater has been installed, and the hoop like smokebox front plate is in position which will form a frame for the smokebox wrapper plate yet to be added. *Courtesy, National Railway Museum, York*

Below left: A 'Claughton' in advanced state of construction, with three more directly behind. The rocking levers in front of the steam chests normally concealed, are clearly seen.

Adjacent inside and outside cylinders together comprised a single casting weighing approximately $2\frac{1}{4}$ tons, two of which were bolted together down the vertical centre line of the locomotive. *Courtesy, National Railway Museum, York*

Above: About 1922 'Claughton' No 2366 underwent indicator trials, although no data now appears to survive.

Below: LNWR 'Renown' class 4-4-0 No 1913 *Canopus* pilots 'Claughton' 4-6-0 No 5933 on the up 'Irish Mail' near Tamworth in 1927. *F. R. Hebron/Rail Archive Stephenson*

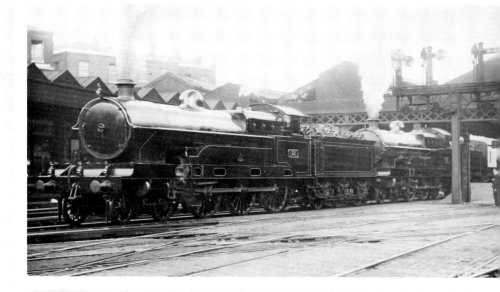

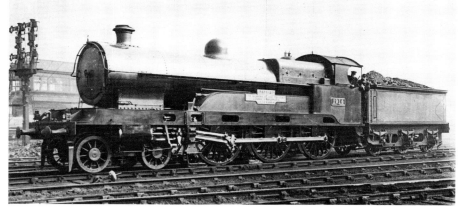

Left: MR Class 2P 4-4-0 No 385 pilots an unidentified 'Claughton' on the down 'Devonian' near Duffield c1930. *F. G. Hebron/Rail Archive Stephenson*

Top: A pair of 'Claughtons' provide a stirring spectacle as they depart from Euston with the Royal Train, c1923.

Above: The classic view of No 1914 *Patriot* at Crewe. *LPC*

Below: One of the first batch of 'Claughtons' No 1161 *Sir Robert Turnbull* displays the slightly apologetic appearance presented by the class, due to the relatively small boiler diameter and setting back of the chimney behind the bogie centre line. *LPC*

7
The 'Claughtons' after 1922

For all their imperfections Bowen Cooke's 'Claughtons' were the largest and most powerful express passenger locomotives to be inherited in substantial numbers by the London, Midland & Scottish Railway upon its formation on 1 January 1923. At this date the most recently built was only 18 months old, and the average age for the 130 strong class was but 4¼ years. However, the design itself dated back a decade to a very different era of cheap fuel and abundant labour, and many of the older examples were still suffering from arrears of maintenance as a result of the effects of World War 1.

The class was renumbered 5900-6029 Derby-style by the new regime, and the seal was set upon the new order by the emergence from Crewe Works in July 1923 of 'Claughton' No 2511, but now LMS No 5971 and named *Croxteth*, resplendent in former Midland Railway crimson lake livery. Much has been made of the alleged reluctance of Crewe Works in the early LMS era to paint engines red, but a realistic explanation is that this time the Works was undergoing complete reorganisation, as a result of which very few locomotives received full repaints. This is not to say strong reluctance in this direction did not exist, but such understandable partisan feelings were constructively channelled into a series of competitive locomotive trials during 1923-1925, which involved representative locomotive designs of Crewe, Derby and Horwich, and to a lesser extent St Rollox origin.

These initially took place over the ex-Midland Leeds-Carlisle route, using the former LYR Dynamometer Car. At the close of 1924 representing the former LNWR was 'Claughton' No 2221 *Sir Francis Dent* which competed against no fewer than three Derby Compound 4-4-0s, and Pickersgill Caledonian Railway 4-4-0 No 124. Respective power classifications were 5P, 4P and 3P and so it was scarcely a contest between equals, and the St Rollox product not being able to keep time with 300 tons was tested no further. With 350 ton trains the results of the jousting between the representatives of Crewe and Derby can be summarised thus:

	MR 4-4-0s Nos 1023 1065 & 1066	LNWR 4-6-0 No 2221
Mileage out of shops	15,031 (average)	23,825
Max DBHP	834 at 52mph (average)	953 at 43mph
Coal consumption		
lb/mile	44.7 (average)	56.4
lb/DBHP hr	4.42 (average)	5.03

From Edge Hill No 2221 was not on the best of form, being plagued throughout the trials by poor steaming. This only served to enhance the evidently greater economy displayed by the Compounds, which despite their greatly inferior adhesive weight did not suffer unduly from slipping.

A few months later, in May 1925, further competitive running took place over Shap between Preston and Carlisle. On this occasion, except for the inevitable Derby Compounds, the contestants were all 4-6-0s, LNWR 'Prince' and 'Claughton', and a Hughes superheated 'Dreadnought'. The 'Claughton', this time No 30 *Thalaba*, returned a slightly improved coal consumption of 4.75lb/DBHP hr, which was also better than that achieved by the other 4-6-0s. More extensive details of these particular trials are given in Chapter 9.

That there was still room for considerable improvement with the 'Claughtons' was obvious, as it had been to Bowen Cooke a decade earlier. There was a double irony in the fact that whereas Derby held that relatively minor alterations to the detail design were all that was required, Crewe, who had designed, built and nurtured the engines considered drastic rebuilding was necessary. Seemingly paradoxically, both were correct. Fundamentally elegant in conception, the 'Claughton' was marred by poor detailed design in its actual execution. Derby was to achieve considerable enhancement in thermodynamic performance by inexpensive conventional alterations within the existing fabric. This equalled in efficiency improvements wrought by Crewe via the use of new cylinders and boilers, but the poor mechanical performance of the class remained, and in the end this was for Derby to solve allied to Crewe's new design of boiler.

In December 1924 an Italian, Arturo Caprotti, delivered a paper to the Institution of Locomotive Engineers in London on his newly devised system of steam distribution to cylinders utilising poppet valves. Beames subsequently obtained dynamometer car test data of an Italian 2-6-2 tender locomotive so fitted, and was presumably sufficiently impressed to get Crewe Drawing Office to prepare drawings for new poppet valve cylinders for the 'Claughtons'. This was carried out in collaboration with William Beardmore & Co who had acquired the British licence to manufacture components to Caprotti's patents, which also concerned marine and stationary engines. One of the initial batch of 'Claughtons', by now LMS No 5908 *Alfred Fletcher* was fitted up in mid-1926.

Comparisons were made with a standard 'Claughton' outshopped simultaneously, No 5917, between 1 January and 18 September 1927. The resultant fuel economy was dramatic:

	Miles run	Coal consumed (tons)	Coal consumption lb/mile (inc lighting & shed duties)
Poppet valve No 5908	33,543	692.0	46.2
Piston valve No 5917	31,970	832.25	58.3

Over the longer period, 1 August 1926 to 18 September 1927, oil consumption was as follows:

	Cylinders (pints)	Motion (pints)	Total	Mileage	Pints per 1,000 miles
No 5908	900	1,657	2,557	48,478	0.053
No 5917	1,620	1,879	3,499	42,886	0.0805

Meanwhile, at Derby drawings had been prepared for detailed modifications to the 'Claughton' boiler, which consisted of:

(1) A reduced number (125) of firetubes increased diameter (2⅛in) with increased water spaces between them.
(2) Increased air space through the firegrate, and improved damper arrangement.
(3) Modified firebrick arch and firehole door.

These modifications were incorporated in No 5923, which had commenced experimental running on the Midland Division in 1926. This engine was also given piston valves with plain rings, in place of the standard LNWR-pattern Trick-ported double admission valves. (Five 'Claughtons' had also been experimentally fitted with Horwich-type piston valves with ball compression release valves in 1923.)

During January-February 1927, Nos 5908, 5917 and 5923 were tested against each other and against Compound No 1073 over the Euston-Crewe-Carlisle route. On all counts the superiority wrought by the Caprotti valve gear was marked, and the LMS test report remarked with ill-concealed glee that on a coal consumption per DBHP hr basis No 5908 had all but equalled (with 320 tons) the 3.8lb achieved by the GWR four-cylinder 4-6-0 No 5000 *Launceston Castle* (with 430 tons) running between Crewe and Carlisle to the same schedule a few weeks earlier during November 1926. The GWR engine's coal *and* water consumption *per mile* was notably greater than any of the four engines, however, presumably being mainly attributable to its relatively low degree of superheat, and also its heavier loading.

No 5923 with its Derby modifications achieved at considerably lower cost, was also a close contender. These purely conventional alterations would have been technically feasible in 1913, and if incorporated in the 'Claughtons' from new could have saved around 200 tons of coal per engine *per annum*, or approaching one quarter of a million tons of fuel by 1927.

By the time Derby issued their report on the comparative trials in May 1927, Crewe Drawing Office had already been working on the design of a new enlarged boiler for the 'Claughtons' for at least six months. This has frequently wrongly been ascribed to Derby and in fact incorporated 5¼in diameter flues, whereas Derby invariably specified 5⅛in to the detriment of the later Stanier 4-6-2s. Occasionally referred to as Scheme 3, the new boiler was indeed more generally designated G9½S in Derby parlance and made its debut on No 5999 *Vindictive* in April 1928. This boiler, with sloping throatplate, was pressed to 200lb, and although only 3in greater in diameter than its predecessor, *appeared* to be very much larger on account of the very short chimney which reduced the maximum height above rail from 13ft 4½in to 12ft 9¾in.

Twenty 'Claughtons' were swiftly rebuilt with the new boiler before the end of the year. Ten of these retained their original cylinders, but nine were additionally rebuilt with Caprotti valve gear. This initially differed from that on No 5908, which was also rebuilt with a larger boiler in December 1928, in that the valves were steam in place of spring operated. Breakages in the operating mechanism, however, soon resulted in a reversion to spring operation, and other lesser problems were also ultimately overcome.

The Caprotti 'Claughtons' were normally worked on a comparatively full regulator, at cut-offs down to 12 per cent, below which there was noticeable knocking and the boilers would not steam. Above 40 per cent cut-off the blast was very strong, although on five engines the cranks were set at 135 degrees, SR 'Lord Nelson' fashion, in order to give eight exhaust beats per revolution. No direct comparison of the large boilered 'Claughtons' (re-classified 5X) against the original design was ever made, but tests *were* conducted between Euston and

		LMS 4-4-0 No 1073	Ex-LNWR 4-6-0s		Caprotti No 5908	GWR 4-6-0 No 5000
			Standard No 5917	Modified No 5923		
Mileage since repair		26,218	12,506	20,521	12,678	new 9/1926
Coal consumption:						
lb/mile		34.1	44.5	40.0	33.3	53.0
lb/DBHPL/hr		3.78	4.86	4.04	3.82	3.78
Water consumption:						
gallon/mile		29.5	31.8	28.2	26.9	36.05
lb/lb coal		8.62	6.96	7.06	8.08	6.80

'Claughton' Test Performance, Crewe-Carlisle
1913 & 1927

			LNWR No 1159 343/360 tons 4 Nov 1913			LMS No 5908 315.6 tons 25 Jan 1927			LMS No 5917 315.6 tons 8 Feb 1927		LMS No 5923 319.6 tons 1 Feb 1927	
miles		Sched.	min	sec	Sched.	min	sec	min	sec	min	sec
0.0	Crewe	0	0	00	0	0	00	0	00	0	00
24.0	Warrington	27	23	15	27	26	20	28	37	28	52
35.8	Wigan	40	34	15	41	38	30	42	9	42	33
39.1	Standish	44	37	30	45	43	10	47	47	46	56
51.0	Preston	58	49	15	60	55	40	61	54	60	18
72.0	Lancaster	81	70	00	83	80	21	85	12	85	08
78.3	Carnforth	88	75	30	89	85	59	91	00	90	51
91.1	Oxenholme	101	88	15	104	100	41	105	49	105	30
104.2	Tebay	117	103	45	121	118	31	124	35	122	44
109.7	Shap Summit	127	110	15	132	128	50	134	21	132	18
123.3	Penrith	141	124	30	146	142	06	147	50	146	19
141.1	Carlisle	159	142	30	158	158	04	165	53	165	22

| | Signal Checks | | Grayrigg 98.2 miles | | None | | Copenhall Junction 2.0 miles | | Copenhall Junction 2.0 miles |

Manchester early in 1931, with a 5X of each variety in order to evaluate the new Derby *three*-cylinder renewal of No 5902 with G9½S boiler. By this time the large-boilered piston valve engines had been fitted with multiple narrow valve rings, and the piston valve engine (No 5910) actually displayed some superiority in fuel consumption over the Caprotti returning 3.27lb/DBHP hr as against 3.53lb. Arguably the most impressive variants of the 'Claughton' breed, a final appraisal of the Caprottis made in April 1935 was inconclusive as to their merits, other than conceding that they maintained a given level of efficiency over a longer period then their piston valve counterparts.

The large-boilered 'Claughtons' were concentrated at specific sheds initially Longsight, Preston and Holyhead. The Caprottis in particular being Beames' special favourites, they were put on high mileage diagrams and therefore by simple arithmetic returned a lower repair cost per mile under the revealing locomotive accountancy procedures inaugurated under Lord Stamp in 1927.

Derby continued to persevere with low cost remedies by using new hollow piston valves carrying narrow rings, and experimenting with the newly developed Finnish Kylala exhaust in association with a larger diameter chimney. Initially fitted to No 5973 the equipment was soon transferred to No 6001, only 11,000 miles out of shops. The latter was tested with and without the Kylala exhaust between Leeds and Carlisle during May-June 1930. With the new-style exhaust No 6001 was noticeably more free-steaming, but with the standard arrangement restored was more economical in fuel. It was therefore deduced the stronger blast produced by the experimental arrangement slightly increased the combustion rate, but that this was counterbalanced by a lower evaporation of water per pound of coal. With original boiler and standard exhaust No 6001 achieved the almost unbelievable coal consumption of 3.6lb/DBHP hr.

Leeds-Carlisle trials, May-June 1930

	No 6001		No 5973
	11,111		35,894
Mileage since last repair	Kylala	Standard	Standard
Type of exhaust			
Coal consumption:			
lb/mile	38.25	35.6	46.35
lb/DBHP hr	3.94	3.63	4.67
Water consumption:			
gallon/mile	29.7	29.4	34.9
lb/lb coal	7.74	8.26	7.58

The Kylala equipment and the distinctive associated chimney subsequently appeared on No 5912 early in 1932. Despite Derby's experiences with the Kyl*ala* equipment on a small-boilered Claughton, late in 1931 Crewe prepared drawings for the fitting of a *single* Kyl*chap* exhaust to a large-boilered Claughton. This duly appeared on No 5975 by which time the gesture was merely academic, the Stanier era had begun.

The new found improvements came too late in the day in that the 'Claughtons' were by this time displaced from pride of place by the new 'Royal Scots', which established entirely new standards of thermodynamic and mechanical efficiency on the LMS. The latter's arrival had permitted the drafting of 25 'Claughtons' (with the original boiler) to the Midland Division during 1928-30. Stringent weight limitations and a decidedly conservative management had resulted in no 4-6-0s previously working over the Derby Empire on a regular basis. The Bridge Stress Committee had, however, discovered that of the 125 locomotive designs tested during the 1920s the 'Claughton' alone was truly perfectly balanced and delivered nil hammerblow at 6 rps.

The 'Claughtons' sent to the Midland Division were all given 4,000gal ROD tenders of Great Central design, which had originally started life behind the 2-8-0s purchased by the LNWR after World War 1. Cabs were also trimmed, and initially the chimneys on some engines were cut down. This adversely affected steaming and their full stature was restored. (Interestingly after 1930 on a number of occasions unrebuilt 'Claughtons' worked through to Edinburgh Princes Street). They were distributed between Kentish Town, Leeds Holbeck and Carlisle Durran Hill sheds, and over the arduous Leeds-Carlisle route with their high adhesive weight and free running characteristics found some favour with footplate crews. It has been suggested that the Midland Division would hardly have received the pick of the bunch and indeed their mechanical performance was very variable.

In *Chronicles of Steam* (Ian Allan Ltd, 1967) E. S. Cox gives some interesting statistics regarding the availability of 23 unrebuilt 'Claughtons' on the Midland Division during the two month period December 1930 – January 1931. Individual mileage run varied from a mere 948 miles by No 5974 of Kentish Town, which only ventured out on 13 out of 62 possible days, to no less than 13,783 miles by No 6012 allocated to the same depot, which was utilised on 50 days.

Cox was particularly well acquainted with the vicissitudes of the 'Claughtons' in their original form, for in April 1931 he compiled a report which detailed their various ailments, every one of which could be put down to poor detail design. By this time their thermodynamic performance had been improved out of all recognition by relatively simple means, but this was to some extent nullified by high maintenance costs.

The worst feature was the close proximity of the bottom of the firebox foundation ring to the tops of the trailing coupled axleboxes. The oil feed arrangements were therefore very cramped and the lubricant supply eventually became cut off entirely after a period of wear and vibration, which was particularly bad in Crewe engines in general on account of their light and economical construction. During the last six months of 1930 there were 60 cases of hot trailing axleboxes on 'Claughtons', but this could not merely be ascribed to advancing age for it is known to have occurred when the engines were new. The Board of Trade report into the crank axle failure of No 2511 (later LMS No 5971 *Croxteth*) at Castlethorp on 4 December 1922, detailed the engine's history from new in May 1920 to date. This revealed that it had been laid up at Camden for precisely one month from 23 May until 24 June 1922, awaiting a replacement trailing axle. The original had run hot and had therefore been irreparably damaged. At that time the LNWR reckoned a large express locomotive out of traffic lost about £7 per day in contemporary currency.

There were repeated reports of rough riding with the engines settling down at the back end. The first 20 'Claughtons' had originally been turned out with laminated springs beneath the trailing coupled axleboxes, but these were soon abandoned in favour of double coil springs, which were now found to be weak and subject to frequent fracture.

At the front end of the engines, the marine-type big ends with solid bushes rubbed against the valve gear return cranks causing overheating. A new type of return crank began to be fitted, and a start had also been made on providing Derby-style smokebox front plates and doors as the originals were prone to distortion thus permitting the ingress of air.

The extensive iron pipe-work associated with the vacuum brake was subject to continuous leakage. Vacuum was maintained by a pump and maintenance costs were very much higher than on the reboilered Claughtons which carried a Derby-pattern ejector.

Similarly the hand sanding gear gave continuous trouble unlike the steam-sanding on the 5X 'Claughtons'.

Cabs and splashers habitually worked loose. It was recommended that 'in any scheme for rebuilding the engines, the splashers should be done away with and a new cab fitted'. Cox himself has recorded in *Locomotive Panorama* Volume 1 (Ian Allan Ltd, 1965) that Beames several years earlier had proposed to 'de-bag' the 'Claughtons'. Despite all these potential afflictions at least 12 'Claughtons', Nos 5908/56/65/85-6, 6002/4/9/13-4/7/24, were deemed early in 1927 to be in first class running order, and were distinguished by a prominent white letter 'S' high on the cab sides. It is interesting to note that five of these engines received G9½S boilers the following year, and no fewer than 10 dated from 1920-1921.

The heavy fuel consumption of the 'Claughtons' was largely due to the single broad Schmidt piston valve rings. To put this in perspective, however, such was standard British practice up to about 1930; most of the 'Royal Scots' were so endowed when new and displayed similar characteristics of progressively increasing fuel consumption with advancing mileage since last shopping. Narrow ring piston valves were applied to most if not all the 'Claughtons' from 1931, to good effect. A number of engines which retained their original boilers also had these re-tubed with 122 2⅛in tubes on a layout similar to that experimentally applied to No 5923 several years earlier. By this time all the class had continuously sloping grates, and so the thermodynamic performance of the original basic 'Claughton' had been enhanced at low cost, without recourse to expensive new boilers and cylinders.

But the Achilles Heel remained. The mechanical performance of the class was still poor, particularly in association with the trailing coupled axle. This prompted Derby Works in 1930 to completely rebuild two engines, Nos 5902 and 5971, as three-cylinder locomotives with G9½S boilers on 'Royal Scot' lines, an operation described in the next chapter. The outstanding success of these prompted thoughts of 'renewing' all the remaining 107 small-boilered engines over the next few years. Only 40 were nominally rebuilt in this manner, before the advent of William Stanier, late of the GWR, as CME overtook events. The delivery of large numbers of his taper-boiler development of the three-cylinder rebuild permitted wholesale retirement of the small-boilered 'Claughtons' during 1934-5.

At the close of 1934 'Claughtons' were still to be seen on express duties on the Midland Division, amongst them No 5900 *Sir Gilbert Claughton* itself, which latterly worked from Saltley on freight trains to Carlisle before retirement in March 1935. The last 'Claughton' to operate in its original form, ie with original cab and LNW tender, was No 5951 whose final duty was to work the 7.15pm Manchester Exchange-Chester on Saturday, 20 October, 1935. This left No 5984 with cut-down cab and ROD tender which was condemned eight days later.

This event was immediately almost preceded by the condemnation of the first 5X 'Claughton'. The provision of the new boilers had thrown considerable strain on the original light frames both by virtue of their increased weight, and heavier piston loads due to their higher steam pressure. Only four engines remained at the beginning of 1937, but their existence was prolonged by the grave international situation, the final trio being based at Willesden. The last two Caprottis were both condemned in 1941 leaving No 6004 (formerly named *Princess Louise*) which thereafter led something of a charmed life. After the end of the war, by which time it was stationed at Edge Hill, its appearance was recorded in numerous locations, as far apart as Willesden and Carlisle. Early in February 1948 it appeared at Derby and one month later was noted at Buxton, which was possibly the first and only time a 'Claughton' had visited the Derbyshire spa. Still contriving to retain a somewhat grimy red livery originally applied a decade earlier, the end finally came in June 1949, No 6004 having amassed 893,534 miles. This event was almost coincident with the retirement of the last surviving 'Precursor' and 'Prince', and all three stalwarts of a bygone era were lined up outside the old Locomotive Offices at Crewe to be officially photographed. The boiler off No 6004 saw further service on an unrebuilt three-cylinder 'Patriot', a class which nominally extended the 'Claughton' saga into the early 1960s, a quarter of a century after the 'Claughton' as originally conceived by Bowen Cooke became extinct.

Claughton Conversions and Withdrawals 1925-1941
No in service

	4-cyl small boiler PV	4-cyl small boiler Caprotti	4-cyl large boiler Caprotti	4-cyl large boiler PV	3-cyl 5X rebuild
1925	130				
1926	129	1			
1927	129	1*			
1928	110		10	10	
1929	109		10	10	
1930	107		10	10	2
1931	107		10	10	2
1932	83		10	10	17
1933	65		10	10	42
1934	30		10	10	42
1935	0		8	8	42
1936			4	6	42
1937			2	2	42
1938			2	2	42
1939			2	2	42
1940			2	1	42
1941			0	1	42

Dates to year ending 31 December
*Rebuilt to large boiled Caprotti, 1928

Small-boilered 'Claughtons' after 1922

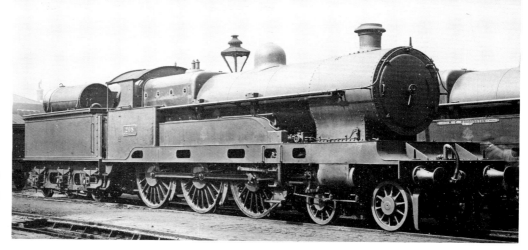

Above left: Immaculate in fully lined crimson lake nameless No 5996 stands at Crewe. *Real Photographs*

Centre left: Although bearing its LMS number on the tender, the latter still retains its LNWR-style lining, as No 6023 hurries past Kenton on an up express. *Real Photographs*

Below left: Some of the finest action photographs of 'Claughtons' in the early LMS era were secured by the late F. R. Hebron. Here No 5944 makes a truly breathtaking sight taking water at Bushey troughs with the LNWR Royal Train on 15 August 1925. Although the locomotive is no more, several vehicles in the formation are now preserved in the National Collection, most of them recently restored to LNWR livery. *F. R. Hebron/Rail Archive Stephenson*

Above right: No 208, still in LNWR livery, fitted up for oil burning on the Scarab system during the Miner's Strike of 1926. *Ian Allan Library*

Right: Another oil burner, this time No 5950, passes Hatch End with the 4pm Euston–Liverpool express. Several of the vehicles are still in LNW livery.

Below: No 5955 provided with cut-down cab and ROD-type tender heads a down cattle train near Elstree. *Real Photographs*

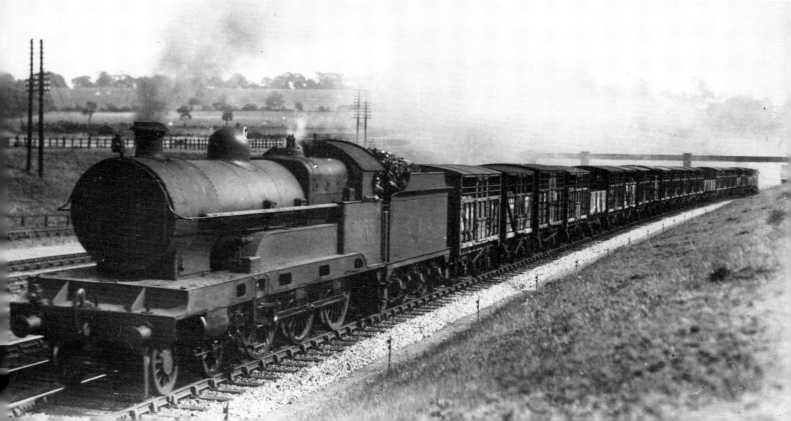

Deviations from Standard

Above left: No 6001 fitted with Kylala exhaust and MR-style chimney at Nottingham Midland. The engine has also acquired a Derby style smokebox door (not fitted during the 1930 tests). *J. P. Wilson Collection*

Left: Another 'Claughton' with improved smokebox door, No 5980 makes a spirited onslaught on Camden bank. A few 'Prince' 4-6-0s were also similarly modified. *Ian Allan Library*

Top: Some Western Division 'Claughtons' also received shortened chimneys, whilst retaining domes of normal stature. Some assistance with smoke lifting was clearly thought to be necessary as evidenced by this view of No 5943. *Real Photographs*

Above right: No 5912 *Lord Faber* with cut down cab and boiler mountings and fitted with a ROD-type tender, immaculate in crimson lake livery at Derby.

Right: 'Claughton' No 5930 *G. R. Jebb* heads the up 'Welshman' along the North Wales coast near Mostyn. *Real Photographs*

Above: The first of the 70 postwar 'Claughtons' was named *Patriot* in commemoration of the LNWR men who gave their lives during World War 1. Newly built No 1914 is seen in its stride on Camden bank on a heavy down express.

Left: A decade later in June 1931 as LMS No 5964 *Patriot* is seen at Bletchley on an up Manchester express. For several years stationed at Rugby the engine formed the centre piece of a ceremony there on Remembrance Sunday. *P. Ransome-Wallis*

Below left: An unidentified 'Claughton' hauls a down Manchester express near Pinner. The engine does not appear to have acquired a full LMS repaint, but carries the company crest on the cab side sheets and the coveted white letter 'S' higher up, dating the photograph at around 1927.

Above right: The 'Claughtons' rated red livery to the end. Here No 5937, one of the last 'Claughtons' to remain substantially in original condition, is seen at Willesden in September 1933. *E. R. Wethersett Collection*

Right: An unidentified 'Claughton' heads the 4pm ex-Euston at Camden. *E. R. Wethersett Collection*

Claughtons under Repair

Left: An unidentified 'Claughton' about to be wheeled in the Erecting Shop at Crewe, c1930, in the foreground lies a second 'Claughton' 'bogie'. *Brian Reed Collection*

Below left: 'Claughton' No 5973 photographed on the wheeldrop at Bedford Shed in August 1932. No 'Claughton' was ever stationed at Bedford, where for a period several of the class showed a marked propensity to run hot on down trains and would have soon found themselves on the wheeldrop. *Crown Copyright, National Railway Museum, York*

Above right: Newly rebuilt with G9½S boiler and immaculate in red livery nameless No 5986 poses at Crewe. *Ian Allan Library*

Right: Not all the large-boilered 'Claughtons' were turned out in red livery. A curious example was No 5953 *Buckingham* which re-appeared in plain black, but whose tender as late as October 1928 still retained LNW lining!

Below: An interesting combination at Crewe, newly-reboilered No 5970 *Patience* pilots small-boilered No 5930 *G. R. Jebb* in May 1928.

Left: No 6017
Breadalbane with ROD-type
tender at speed near Tring.
E. R. Wethersett

**Below left: In the wake of
similar modifications to the
'Royal Scots', from 1932 the
large-boilered 'Claughtons'
with their short chimneys
were provided with smoke
deflectors, as shown in this
view of No 5953**
Buckingham.
Real Photographs

**Below: As with the 'Patriots',
the top edges of the smoke
deflectors were later slightly
turned inwards. No 6004 at
Willesden Shed in July 1939.**
Courtesy J. P. Wilson

**Right: No 6004 was destined
to be the last surviving
'Claughton'. Only two others,
both Caprottis, were still in
service when this view of
No 6004 heading the 6.15
Camden-Birmingham Goods
in June 1939 was taken at
Kilburn. Remarkably the
engine was still to see all but
10 years' further service.**
E. R. Wethersett

The Caprotti 'Claughtons'

Above left: Retaining its original boiler, No 5908 *Alfred Fletcher* was rebuilt with Caprotti poppet valve gear in mid-1926. It is seen here amid sylvan surroundings at Crewe in February 1927 its tender devoid of insignia, but its cab side bearing the coveted 'S' which denoted first class mechanical condition.

Left: No 6013 with Caprotti valve gear hauls the up 'Lancastrian' over Castlethorpe troughs in June 1931. When newly rebuilt the Caprotti 'Claughtons' achieved a 32% greater annual mileage than their large-boilered piston valve counterparts. *L. J. Thompson*

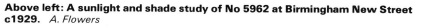

Above left: A sunlight and shade study of No 5962 at Birmingham New Street c1929. *A. Flowers*

Top: The four cranks of five of the 10 Caprotti 'Claughtons' were set at 135 degrees in order to give eight exhaust beats per revolution. One of these, distinguished by enlarged balance weights, is seen at Llandudno in June 1933. *G. H. F. Atkins*

The final development of the 'Claughton' in four-cylinder form was the provision in 1932 of single Kylechap exhaust on large-boilered Caprotti No 5975 *Talisman* (135 degree crank setting). (Above) Newly converted, No 5975 on shed. (Left) Sporting the later style of smoke deflectors enters Crewe on a down express which includes some early Stanier stock. *V. Forster*

Croxteth

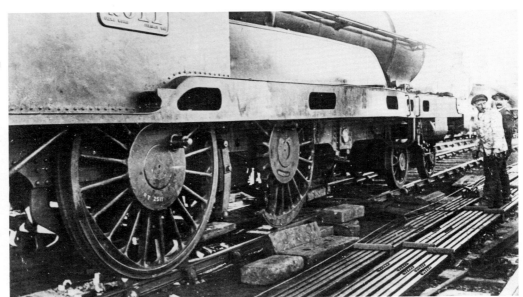

Right: 'Claughton' No 2511 after suffering a crank axle failure near Castlethorpe whilst hauling the 10.20am Euston-Liverpool on 4 December 1922.

Below: After undergoing the necessary repairs the engine duly reappeared in the summer of 1923 as the first LNWR locomotive to be repainted in Derby crimson lake livery by the newly formed LMS. It was now LMS No 5971 and was given the time honoured LNWR name of *Croxteth*. This official view, dated 7 August 1923, clearly shows the ultimate pattern of LNWR self-trimming tender, with square ended frame introduced in 1916.
Courtesy, National Railway Museum, York

Right: *Croxteth* was clearly accident prone. It was damaged beyond economic repair by colliding head on with a stationary ballast train in a tunnel near Culgaith, whilst hauling a Hellifield-Carlisle passenger train on the Midland Division on 6 March 1930. The main frames, described as 'badly buckled' in the official report, are here seen in Derby Works awaiting incorporation in a so-called rebuild.

Above: No 5971 was nominally rebuilt as a three-cylinder locomotive with G9½S boiler late in 1930, and returned to Leeds Holbeck Shed. Initially it was not fitted with smoke deflectors and is here seen in this comparatively short-lived form.

Left: No 5971 still nameless but fitted with smoke deflectors, at Nottingham Midland station. The distinctive coupled wheel centres with large centre bosses are clearly seen. The name *Croxteth*, borne on curved cast brass nameplates, was restored prior to renumbering to 5500 in May 1934. *G. H. F. Atkins*

Below left: No 5500 was renamed *Patriot* in February 1937 and is seen at Willesden Shed in July 1939. *J. P. Wilson*

Below: In its final form as BR No 45500 in BR green, beneath the grime, at Birmingham New Street, in October 1959. The engine was withdrawn from service 18 months later in March 1961 with 1,239,904 miles to its credit since 'conversion' to three-cylinder propulsion.

8
The 'Patriots'

The death knell of the 'Claughtons' was sounded a few weeks *before* a member of the class, No 5927, met an abrupt and untimely end in a collision with a goods train on the Midland Division at Doe Hill on 12 February 1929, when it was written off as being beyond economic repair. In November 1928 Derby Drawing Office had conceived a scheme whereby the 'Claughtons' would be renewed with *three* cylinders and the Crewe-designed G9½S boiler.

Initially it was considered employing Lentz oscillating cam valve gear, but soon a more practical decision to employ standard 'Royal Scot' cylinders and valve gear prevailed and design work proceeded at Derby during 1929. Towards the end of that year Derby Works began construction of 20 further 'Royal Scots', although the formal authorisation for these does not appear to have been granted until around the time the first examples were already running trials! On 6 March 1930 another 'Claughton' had been severely damaged in a collision, this time at Culgaith in Westmorland, the locomotive concerned being none other than No 5971 *Croxteth*. The official report of the accident described the frames of the engine as having been badly buckled, but these were nevertheless in part utilised in a three-cylinder renewal subsequently assembled to the new drawings at Derby. As on many LNWR locomotive classes, the front section of the main frames adjacent to the cylinders was cut separately from the rear section to which it was lap jointed between the 'bogie' and leading coupled axle. The new three-cylinder No 5971, along with No 5902 renewed simultaneously, therefore preserved the old Claughton coupled wheel spacing of 7ft 5in + 7ft 10in.

Most noticeable, however, was the retention of the original coupled wheel centres with large centre bosses. Also utilised were the original double radial trucks with curved slide and lacking centre pivot, of which precisely the same design was incidentally used at the trailing end of the large Beames 0-8-4 tanks.

Nos 5902 and 5971 emerged from Derby during November 1930 in immediate succession to the 20 'Royal Scots' just completed there. Their boilers appear to have been appropriated from a batch of five built at Crewe in 1929 possibly with the thought of reboilering further 'Claughtons', no spares having been built for the 20 1928 conversions. The tenders were second hand, and the two rebuilds initially ran nameless and without smoke deflectors. In appearance Nos 5902 and 5971 approximated to how a Midland Railway 4-6-0 *might* have looked had Derby felt so inclined in say 1922. It is only fair to add that at around that time locomotive design activity at Derby was at a low level, and in any case there was a substantial Crewe element in the new ensemble. Much involved in the mechanical design of the three-cylinder rebuilds was Jack Francis, the best of the Crewe design team, who before transfer to Derby had been responsible for the G9½S boiler.

Here at last then was evidence of a happy measure of co-operation between Derby and Crewe, although the ancestry of

Nos 5902 and 5971 was decidedly complex, also owing much to the 'Royal Scot' whose own origins have been hotly debated. The 'Scots' in turn were allegedly inspired, so it is said, by the Maunsell Southern 'Lord Nelsons' which likewise were influenced by GWR practice, but which in the style of their cabs and tenders at least bore the hallmarks of Derby owing to the influence of James Clayton, who had left the Midland Railway to join Maunsell at Ashford in 1913.

When only three months old in February 1931 No 5902 was tested on normal service trains between Euston and Manchester against representative piston valve and Caprotti 5X 'Claughtons', which yielded the following results with circa 400ton trains:

	No 5902 3-cylinder	No 5910 4-cylinder	No 5908 4-cylinder
Valve gear	Walschaerts*	Walschaerts*	Caprotti
Coal consumption:			
lb/mile	35.2	38.2	39.9
lb/DBHP hr	3.12	3.27	3.53

Multiple narrow valve rings.

It will be seen that in terms of fuel economy the three-cylinder engine did *not* show a notable improvement, although it did enjoy the advantage of long lap/long travel valves. Its superiority lay in the mechanical field in terms of increased availability and annual mileage.

No 5092 remained on the Western Division whilst No 5971 returned to Leeds for service on the Midland Division, upon which the larger and heavier 'Royal Scots' were barred, and indeed did not normally operate in their original parallel boiler form. Mainly on account of their bad record of the trailing coupled axleboxes in 1931 it was resolved to renew several 'Claughtons' falling due for new boilers and cylinders as three-cylinder 5X engines. Fifteen such were authorised on Stanier's first day in office as CME, 1 January 1932, and began to emerge from Crewe the following July. Not altogether surprisingly in view of their appearance they were quickly popularly referred to as 'Baby Scots'. In fact the phrase might not have been quite so apt, because it would appear that these engines were found to weigh 83.4 tons, as against 84.9 tons for a 'Royal Scot', their *empty* weight actually being slightly the greater of the two. Their weight was accordingly speedily reduced (on paper) to accord with the 80.75 tons of Nos 5902 and 5971!

Altogether 40 renewals were sanctioned for Crewe and Derby, to take the running numbers of the unrebuilt 'Claughtons' they supposedly replaced. These differed from the two 1930 conversions in having 'Royal Scot' coupled axle spacing, 7ft 4in + 8ft 0in, and coupled axleboxes, except that the first 10 utilised 'Claughton' pattern axleboxes and double radial trucks. The remainder got true centre pivot bogies with the same 6ft 3in wheelbase. Although appearing in Stanier's time the design was pre-Stanier in conception, but he was at least able to make these improvements to the majority, although strangely he never fitted his own pattern of chimney.

A further 15 engines, officially regarded as entirely new, were also ordered, to be numbered 6030-6044. Ten of these appeared early in 1934, by which time it had been decided to logically renumber the class from 5500 in order of reconstruction/ construction. Nos 5902 and 5971 had for a time regained their original names on new curved brass nameplates, and now became Nos 5501 and 5500 respectively. In February 1937 the latter was renamed *Patriot* and this then became the official designation for the class, although the term 'Baby Scot', frowned upon in official circles, continued to be used in many quarters.

The five outstanding 'Patriots' on the 1934 Programme were turned out in immediate succession as the first five Stanier three-cylinder 5X 4-6-0s, Nos 5552-5556. These were originally to have been numbered 6040-6044, and a document relating to them bears the interesting handwritten note '38 out of the 58 Rebuilt "Claughtons" on the 1934 Programme to be numbered 6045-6082 inclusive'.

Prior to the designation of the class as the 'Jubilees' in 1935 the Stanier three-cylinder 4-6-0s were officially referred to by such cumbersome titles as 'Taper Boiler Rebuilt Claughtons'. Probably for accountancy reasons some of the early examples did actually incorporate a few minor components from withdrawn 'Claughtons', but not to the extent originally intended and claimed by J. C. Loach in 1948 on p59 of *Journal* No 201 of the *Institution of Locomotive Engineers*. A member of the former LMS technical staff, Loach averred that 12 'Patriots' and 53 'Jubilees' utilised double radial trucks without centre pivots. The arrangement drawing for the 'Claughton' 'bogie' was indeed 'marked up' for 'Patriots' Nos 5500-5511, and the first 53 Crewe-built 'Jubilees', ie Nos 5552-5556 and 5607-5654, but the 'Jubilee' entries were subsequently cancelled. However, these engines *were* turned out with 6ft 3in wheelbase bogies with side bearers which utilised 'Claughton' sideframes and axleboxes, and which could be distinguished from the front by a plate cross stay. The remaining 138 'Jubilees' were given standard 6ft 6in bogies with double coil spring lateral control and side bearers, which were designed at Derby late in 1932 and made their first appearance under the humble 10 '2P' 0-4-4Ts.

These main differences apart the main chassis and running gear of the 'Jubilees' closely followed that of the 'Patriots', the main components of the valve gear and the 9in piston valves themselves being interchangeable with those of the 'Patriots' and 'Royal Scots'. The cylinders however, were of new design being reduced in bore from 18in to 17in, to compensate for the increase in boiler pressure from 200lb to 225lb. The general proportions of the first 'Jubilee' boilers, and the fireboxes in particular, were closely based on those of the GWR 'Castle' class, especially the '5013' series which was underway at Swindon at the time of Stanier's departure for the LMS. (The boiler clothing arrangement drawing, prepared at Derby in October 1932, clearly showed a pure Swindon combined top feed casing and safety valve bonnet. This adornment was suppressed by the time the first Stanier 5X was completed at Crewe 18 months later, following Stanier's chagrin at the provision of such a fitting on his first 2-6-0 in 1933.)

The first comparisons to be made as to the performance of the 'Jubilees' and the 'Patriots' were made during the Autumn of 1934 when dynamometer car tests were conducted between Wolverhampton and Euston, with the last parallel-boilered 'Patriot'-built, No 5551, and taper boiler No 5556. These were instituted primarily to assess capabilities for traffic purposes on the Euston-Birmingham two hour services, and for possible future accelerated timings. Nevertheless fuel and water consumption was also measured, and overall there was very little to choose between the two engines, any slight advantage falling in favour of No 5556.

Wolverhampton-Birmingham-Euston, Autumn 1934

Loco No	No 5551	No 5556
Boiler	Parallel 200lb	Taper 225lb
Mileage from new	24,149	10,000
Coal consumption:		
lb/mile	41.6	40.4
lb/DBHP hr	3.58	3.51
Water consumption:		
gallons per mile	35.6	35.6
lb/lb coal	8.57	8.84

This was surprising not least because steamchest temperatures on No 5551 averaged 550-570°F as against only 490-510°F by No 5556 on account of the latter's small 2-row superheater. Furthermore in everyday service at this time the new Stanier engines were not comparing favourably with the 'Patriots', being plagued with poor steaming. Compared to the GWR Standard No 8 ('Castle') boiler, upon which the original 'Jubilee' boiler was based, owing to the provision of an appreciably lower number of 2in firetubes evaporative heating surface and total free gas area were both substantially reduced, the latter from 15.7 to 13.2 per cent of the grate area. Stanier quickly discovered that the introduction of low degree superheat, GWR-style, on the LMS constituted a major error of judgement. As a result later 'Jubilees' were given 3-row superheaters and a tube/flue arrangement which also provided increased free gas area. Steaming was very much improved but boiler efficiency still did not measure up to that of the 'Patriots'.

This was demonstrated by further tests, which utilised *both* LMS dynamometer cars, No 2 having been provided with an integrator. These tests again took place between Wolverhampton and Euston and involved representative 'Patriots' and 'Jubilees', the latter having both 2-row and 3-row superheaters. The ensuing test report recorded that evaporation by the 3-row taper boiler was 5.7 per cent less than the 'Patriot', and it was observed that 'taking into account the differences in boiler pressure, and assuming the same superheat it may be shown that the efficiency of the parallel boiler is approximately 6 per cent higher than that of the taper boiler'. The cylinder efficiency of the 3-row taper boiler engines was, however, assumed to be superior because specific water consumption was 7.7 per cent *less*. This was not altogether surprising in view of the more recent design of the cylinders and their relatively more generous valve proportions, although during these tests it was noted that under given conditions the 'Jubilees' tended to be worked at a slightly later cut-off. Nevertheless the improved cylinder efficiency of the latter outweighed their inferior boiler efficiency, which resulted in slightly better energy conversion at the drawbar.

Wolverhampton-Birmingham-Euston, April 1935

Loco Nos	5518/5525	5645-6	5556
Boiler	Parallel (G9½S)	Taper (3A)	Taper (3A)
Superheater	3-row	3-row	2-row
Coal consumption:			
lb/mile	38.4	37.0	43.4
lb/DBHP hr	3.41	3.34	3.71
Water consumption:			
gallons/mile	30.8	28.0	35.4
lb/lb coal	8.02	7.56	8.14

By this time a redesign of the 'Jubilee' boiler had already been completed at Derby which was applied to all new engines from No 5665. The firebox was provided with a sloping throatplate and both grate area and free gas area were increased. The regulator was removed from the smokebox to a conventional dome, and the new boiler put the 'Jubilees' well ahead of the 'Patriots', whose built up smokeboxes like those of the 'Royal Scots' could suffer badly from air leaks. The curious total of 191 'Jubilees' was delivered up to the close of 1936, their rapid influx greatly modifying the distribution of the 'Patriots', which was very different in 1938 compared to what it had been only four years earlier. The heyday of the 'Patriots' on the Midland Division was relatively short lived, but although always prominently associated with the Western Division, it is interesting to note that in 1938 three each were also operating on the Central and Northern Division from Newton Heath and Polmadie sheds, thus:

	July 1934	July 1938
Willesden	0	2
Camden	8	13
Bescot	0	1
Bushbury	1	7
Aston	1	7
Crewe	4	0
Edge Hill	3	3
Longsight	4	5
Preston	3	5
Patricroft	4	0
Carlisle	5	0
Kentish Town	9	0
Leeds	8	3
Newton Heath	0	3
Polmadie	2	3

By January 1937 the LMS operated a fleet of 314 three-cylinder 4-6-0s which provided a formidable 'second eleven' to its then meagre stud of 13 wide firebox 4-6-2s. Crewe built the last parallel G10¼S boilers for the 'Scots' in 1938 when Derby examined the possibility of a three-cylinder 4-6-2 with 20ton axleload for the Midland Division. This proposal would appear to have been dropped in favour of a scheme to renew the 'Royal Scots' with taper boilers. The latter were designed at Derby in 1939 being based on that developed at Crewe five years earlier and fitted to No 6170 *British Legion* in 1935. Delayed by the outbreak of war the first 'Scot' conversions did not take place until 1943, some of the earliest being drafted to the Midland Division, upon which they performed sterling work between Leeds and Carlisle.

Not surprisingly in the aftermath of the outstanding trials with 4-6-2 6234 *Duchess of Abercorn* so fitted, plain double exhaust was incorporated in the design of the new boiler and undoubtedly contributed to its subsequent success. Designated 2A, the latter actually made its début on two 'Jubilees', Nos 5735 and 5736, in early 1942. Subsequently all 70 'Royal Scots' and 18 'Patriots' were similarly fitted between 1943 and 1955. Published figures for the 'Scots' indicated a reduction in weight of almost 2 tons, largely achieved through the use of nickel alloy steel plates. Much of this advantage was lost in boilers built after 1946 which utilised normal mild steel, although as with the 'Duchess' 4-6-2s similarly no distinction was ever made on official weight diagrams.

Whereas all the rebuilds also received improved cylinders, the 'Scot' conversions virtually amounted to new engines, getting new coupled wheel centres, and very often new frames also. In 1944 LMS report the frame performance of the 'Scots' was rated as 'very poor', whereas that of the mechanically very similar 'Patriots' was considered in contrast to be 'good'. (Perhaps not entirely unconnected was the fact that the 'Scots' were always notoriously rough riders, especially when due for shops, whereas their smaller brethren were not particularly bad in this respect.) Nevertheless, whereas on the first eight 'Patriot' rebuilds only the front end of their frames was renewed, on the final ten entirely new frames were provided. Some drivers considered the 'Patriot' rebuilds to be superior steamers to the 'Scots'.

Only 18 'Patriots', however, were rebuilt with taper boilers between 1946 and 1949, which did not include any of the initial 12 (Nos 5500-5511) which genuinely incorporated 'Claughton' components. In mid-1949 debate took place as to whether the remainder should also be rebuilt. Although at this time the age of the engines ranged from 15 to 17 years only, it was recommended that several per year should be condemned from 1952 onwards as their boilers fell due for renewal, and be replaced by a like number of the new Class 6 (Clan) two cylinder 4-6-2s, then being designed, for which some justification was evidently being sought. In the event this recommendation was not implemented, possibly because following the early withdrawal of the 5X 'Claughtons' and rebuilding of some 'Patriots' there were, in theory at least, around twice as many G9½S boilers (72 having been constructed) as there were unrebuilt 'Patriots' to carry them. Only 10 'Clans' were built for service in Scotland, and the unrebuilt 'Patriots' survived the 1950s until 1960-1962. Interestingly, four when broken up carried boilers which had started life on the frames of four-cylinder 'Claughtons' in 1928.

Below left: No 5905 *Lord Rathmore*, new at Nottingham c1933. This engine was one of 10 nominal three-cylinder renewals of 'Claughtons' produced at Derby in 1933. The engine was renumbered 5533 in 1934. *G. H. F. Atkins*

Above: LMS 'Patriot' No 5535 *Sir Herbert Walker KCB* heads an up fast goods near Napsbury. *E. D. Bruton*

Right: 'Patriot' No 5996 (later No 5528, named *REME* as late as 1959) heads a down Manchester express at Berkhamsted.
Real Photographs

Below: 'Patriot' No 5510 hauls an up theatrical special, including scenery vans, at Willesden in March 1936. This engine was never named.
E. R. Wethersett

656

This picture: A splendid study of 'Patriot' No 5544 never named, nor rebuilt, leaving Preston in the 1930s. *E. Treacy*

Bottom: 'Patriot' No 5525 *Colwyn Bay* climbs out of Euston with a down Birmingham and Wolverhampton express, as late afternoon shadows lengthen in September 1938. *E. R. Wethersett*

Top: No 5538, with crosshead vacuum pump disconnected, seen at Derby in March 1938, shortly before named *Giggleswick* after the famous Yorkshire school.

Above: In early BR days No 45515 *Caernarvon* climbs Camden bank with a Holyhead express. *E. Treacy*

Below: Two 'Patriots' Nos 45511 *Isle of Man*, and 45524 *Blackpool*, blast past Scout Green during the golden summer of 1949. *F. R. Hebron*

Right: No 45518 *Bradshaw* heads a freight train through Lancaster.
E. Treacy

Left: Shortly before withdrawal No 45543 *Home Guard* was recorded at Patricroft shed in July 1962. *J. R. Carter*

Below left: No 5504 *Royal Signals* heads into the daylight out of Linslade Tunnel. *W. S. Garth*

Below: No 45500 *Patriot* itself, at Willesden in September 1959. *R. A. Panting*

Above right: No 5543 heads the up 'Lancastrian' near Brinklow on 23 September 1937. *T. G. Hepburn/Rail Archive Stephenson*

Centre right: No 5545, which did not receive the name *Planet* until rebuilt in 1948, seen in repose in its original form. *Ian Allan Library*

Below right: No 5523 heads over Bushy troughs with a Birmingham-Euston express in May 1937. This engine was named *Bangor* the following year, although several 'Patriots' for ever remained unnamed, although all those later rebuilt with taper boilers carried nameplates. *E. R. Wethersett Collection*

Right: No 5905 *Lord Rathmore* climbs away from Nottingham towards Edwalton with the up 'Thames-Forth' express. The 22 Midland Division 'Patriots' were transferred to the Western Division as early as the beginning of 1935, following the arrival of the first Stanier '5X' 4-6-0s, many of which displaced them initially with unhappy results.
T. G. Hepburn/Rail Archive Stephenson

Centre right: No 5971 at Nottingham Midland without smoke deflectors. Note that only the backing for the nameplate is in position and not the plate itself.
J. N. Hall/Rail Archive Stephenson

Below right: It is a debatable point whether the overall appearance of the 'Patriots' could have been enhanced by the provision of a different design of chimney. Perhaps this is why Crewe experimentally fitted No 6005 with a McIntosh CR-pattern chimney (purely for photographic purposes) late in 1932. Note also the plain smoke deflectors, and non-standard coupled wheel centres with solid webs adjacent to the crank pins. Other early Crewe-built 'Patriots' also seem to have carried this short lived feature, which was soon replaced by standard 'Royal Scot' pattern wheel centres.
Courtesy, National Railway Museum, York

Below: LMS No 5554, later named *Canada*, one of the first five Stanier 'Jubilees' originally authorised as 'Patriots' (although neither of these class designations was then in use).
Crown Copyright, National Railway Museum, York

Left: Stanier Class 5X 'Jubilee' No 5615 with 6ft 3in bogie, nameless in original condition with flat-sided tender, heads a St Pancras-Manchester express near Scratchwood. *R. F. Hebron*

Below: The first Stanier 5X three-cylinder 4-6-0 No 5552 as newly completed in April 1934. A year later this engine exchanged its running number with No 5642 which was then named *Silver Jubilee*. *Ian Allan Library*

Bottom: No 5555 as newly built, with 6ft 3in bogie and two-row superheater, later named *Quebec* in 1937.

Above: No 5553 pilots NBL–built No 5605 on the up 'Lakes Express' over Bushy troughs. *E. R. Wethersett*

Right: Although designed specifically for rebuilding the 'Royal Scots' the excellent 2A taper boiler actually made its first appearance on two 'Jubilees' in 1942. The first of the two recipients was No 5735 *Comet*, here seen entering Euston on a train of vans from Glasgow in April 1948. *E. D. Bruton*

Below: The Stanier Class 5X in its final form with improved high-superheat domed boiler as exemplified by No 5721 *Impregnable* (Crewe, 1936). *Ian Allan Library*

Bottom: 'Patriot' No 45535 *Sir Herbert Walker KGB* newly converted with a 2A taper boiler in 1948. The rebuilt 'Patriots' and 'Scots' looked particularly well in early BR lined black livery before the provision of smoke deflectors. Whereas the 'Scots' kept their original cabs, the 'Patriots' received new Stanier-pattern cabs. *E. Treacy*

Above: Only eight 'Patriots' received taper boilers prior to nationalisation, and so photographs of them in this guise in LMS livery are not common. Here is No 5526 *Morecambe and Heysham* newly converted at Camden in 1947. *P. Ransome-Wallis*

Left: No 45535 again, adorned with smoke deflectors and carrying BR lined green passenger livery. But for their 6ft 3in bogies and 17in instead of 18in cylinders the rebuilt 'Patriots' were almost mechanically identical with the taper boiler 'Scots'. *G. Clarke*

9
The Hughes 'Dreadnoughts'

The premiership of the 'Claughtons' between Crewe and Carlisle was actually challenged shortly *before* 1923 by another four-cylinder 4-6-0. In basic design this was even older than the 'Claughton', but it had recently been completely modernised in a most impressive manner, and new engines were currently being built to the improved pattern by the Horwich Works of the erstwhile Lancashire & Yorkshire Railway.

Like the North Eastern Railway, whose sphere of operations was also totally remote from the Capital, the LYR was a most progressive enterprise. Both the LYR and NER carried out much pioneering work in suburban railway electrification schemes, which had these operated in the London area, might have received greater credit. The same might also be said of their steam locomotives, for in 1899 the Lancashire & Yorkshire Railway had produced what at that time were the largest express passenger locomotives in Europe, J. A. F. Aspinall's ungainly inside-cylinder 4-4-2s. One of these was early credited with attaining a speed in three figures between Manchester and Liverpool. 117mph was almost impossibly high, but the so-called 'Highfliers' were undoubtedly very fast machines.

E. S. Cox, who joined the LYR as an apprentice at Horwich Works in 1917, has said of the 4-4-2s that they could 'run but not pull', whereas the later Hughes 4-6-0s could 'pull but not run'. In view of the severe gradients and frequent stops on the close knit LYR system the 4-4-2s with their 7ft 3in coupled wheels would appear to have been a most unsuitable type, but in fact were very successful. Such could not be said of the Hughes 4-6-0s in their original form, 20 of which had been authorised with some urgency in February 1907 in order to cope with increasing train weights and faster schedules.

Unusually for a locomotive of those times, their designer made public shortly after their appearance the thinking which had gone into their design and the various features adopted, not to say operational difficulties subsequently encountered, in a detailed paper presented to the Institution of Civil Engineers in March 1909.* Hughes was possibly second only to Churchward on the Great Western Railway regarding his scientific attitude to locomotive testing, and his 4-6-0s both in their original, and particularly in their later superheated form, were subjected to more extensive road testing than any other class of British locomotive before 1923.

Hughes was also second only to Churchward in experimenting with the Schmidt high degree superheater in 1906. Churchward subsequently opted for low degree superheat in conjunction with long travel piston valves, but in 1909 Hughes rebuilt four 4-4-0s with high degree superheat and long travel piston valves. Regrettably he did not persevere with the latter feature and concentrated his efforts on evolving various effective patterns of superheater. The design of his original 4-6-0s and their

* 'Locomotives Designed and Built at Horwich Works' by George Hughes.

construction during 1907-9 was unfortunate in that this occurred between the initial superheater experiments on two 0-6-0s, and the subsequent adoption of the equipment as standard (in various forms) from 1911.

If the LNWR 'Claughtons' were amongst the first entirely new British express passenger locomotives to be designed around the superheater, then the Hughes 4-6-0s were amongst the last to be built with saturated boilers and slide valves. The latter were operated by Joy valve gear, which was also favoured by Horwich, and which was located between the frames operating the inside valves directly, and those of the outside cylinders by means of rocking levers. As such the valve gear on the original Hughes 4-6-0s must have been a fitter's nightmare.

Hughes' paper revealed that as built these engines suffered a common failing of Edwardian 4-6-0s in that the close proximity of the firebox foundation ring to the trailing coupled axle severely restricted the access of air to the rear section of the firegrate, where combustion became poor. This was to some extent successfully overcome by providing an air trunk which connected both ends of the ashpan by passing *beneath* the trailing axle. At the front end of the boiler poor steaming had necessitated considerable experimentation with the draughting arrangements which were ultimately drastically revised with the provision of increased blastpipe and noticeably enlarged chimney diameter. The latter modification was also made to the big 0-8-2 shunting tanks which had immediately preceded the 4-6-0s. These had a very similar but slightly shorter boiler of the same maximum outside diameter, ie 5ft 9½in, which was then virtually a British record.

The massive proportions of the LYR 4-6-0s quickly earned them the nickname of the 'Dreadnoughts', the period of their construction coinciding almost exactly with increasing public hysteria as to the accelerating naval arms race with Imperial Germany. Hughes made considerable play of the careful balancing techniques employed and made no secret of the true weights of his masterpiece. Only nine months earlier when No 1506 had been completed in June 1908, a weight diagram had been forwarded to the North Eastern Chief Engineer at York which gave only the *estimated* weights. This indicated an anticipated total weight, less the diminutive six-wheeled tender of but 72½ tons, with 18½ tons resting upon each coupled axle. In fact the actual total weight was found to be just over 77 tons, and the maximum axleload was 19.8 tons, giving a high weight per foot run for that period.

This discrepancy may explain why the NER quickly clamped an embargo upon the LYR 4-6-0s working over their metals from Goole into Hull. The ban was eventually lifted, and it was not until c1919 that Low Moor 4-6-0s appeared in Leeds. Hughes claimed that his 4-6-0s had been designed to be powerful and compact, with powers of rapid acceleration, with the intention of hauling both passenger and certain express goods trains. In

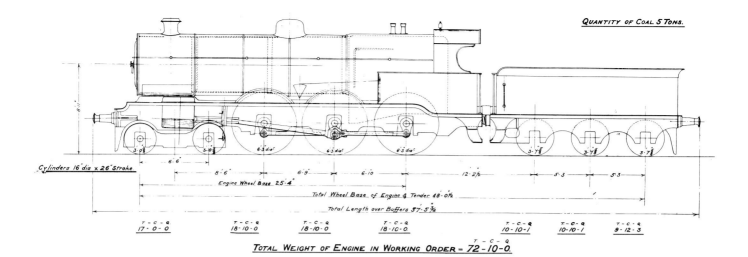

Cylinders 16″ dia × 26″ Stroke

Engine Wheel Base 25′ 4″

Total Wheel Base of Engine & Tender 48′-0½

Total Length over Buffers 57′-5¾

| T-C-Q 17-0-0 | T-C-Q 18-10-0 | T-C-Q 18-10-0 | T-C-Q 18-10-0 | T-C-Q 10-10-1 | T-C-Q 10-10-1 | T-C-Q 9-12-3 |

TOTAL WEIGHT OF ENGINE IN WORKING ORDER = 72-10-0.

Above: Weight diagram of original saturated steam design showing (under) estimated weights (1908).

Below: Contrast in front ends. (Left) The final series of Hughes 4–6–0. Clearly apparent is the 'top and bottom' superheater, and cladding of the smokebox. (Right) Front end arrangement applicable to the first 60 LNWR 'Claughtons' built during 1913–1917. In the 70 engines built during 1920–1921 the superheater dampers were discarded, the blastpipe nozzle lowered, and the long continuous chimney liner superseded by a secondary petticoat pipe. This latter arrangement was regarded as standard by 1926.

heavy joint LYR/NER Newcastle-Liverpool trains, which the LYR worked south of York. The 4-6-0s were allowed to take up to 450 tons through to York, and over the steeply graded Great Central line from Penistone to Sheffield Victoria, as against 340 tons by the 4-4-2s. The official loading tables also indicated that the 4-6-0s enjoyed a distinct advantage on the Holmfirth branch!

Compared to that of other major railway companies our knowledge of the design, development and operation of the locomotives of the Lancashire & Yorkshire Railway would be slender indeed but for the writings of the late Eric Mason. Starting his long railway career as an apprentice at Horwich Works about 1913 Mason was possessed of an encyclopaedic knowledge of the LYR and its locomotives, which he encapsulated in his definitive *The Lancashire & Yorkshire Railway in the Twentieth Century* (Ian Allan Ltd, 1954). Mason's personal records dated back to 1908 and he was closely acquainted with the Hughes 4-6-0s throughout their existence. In his book he recalled the occasion in July 1913 when two of them were called upon to haul the LNWR Royal Train during the course of a visit by King George V to

practice they were notably sluggish, and rarely if ever were to be found on freight duties.

Despite the advantage of 70 per cent greater adhesive weight and a commensurate increase in tractive effort the 4-6-0s did not compare particularly well with the earlier 4-4-2s. It was generally reckoned that the former only really came into their own on the

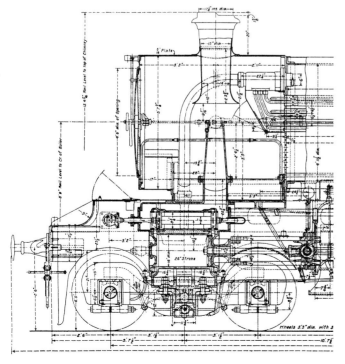

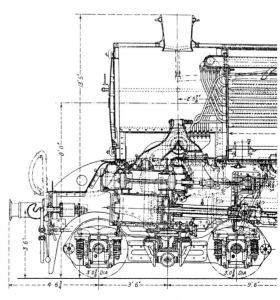

Lancashire. No 1514 alone initially hauled His Majesty from Blackpool Talbot Road to Rainford Halt, but the following day *both* No 1514 and No 1525 hauled the Royal Train from thence to Colne. Mason claimed that this precaution was taken because of the lack of water troughs over the 76½ mile route, for which purpose both engines were temporarily given 3,600gal eight-wheeled tenders off 0-8-0s, in place of their own small 2,480gal six-wheelers.

This could well have been partly the case, but reference to the Log of the Hughes Dynamometer Car is revealing. Two weeks before the Royal Visit No 1514 had made a dress rehearsal run with LYR stock and the Dynamometer Car aggregating 294½ tons, to emulate the LNWR Royal Train, and lost 8min 56sec on the schedule between Rainford Halt and Colne. Eight days later a repeat run was made with both Nos 1514 and 1525 and 3min were *gained* on the schedule!

Rather strangely in his book Mason makes no reference whatever to the Hughes Dynamometer Car, which had been completed at Newton Heath in 1912 modelled on a Belgian prototype inspected during the course of a visit by senior LYR officers to Belgium the previous year. This vehicle made its maiden trip on 7 February 1913 behind the pioneer 4-6-0 No 1506 from Horwich to Hellifield, via Bolton, returning via Chorley. Some months later, between July and October, No 1506 made a series of test runs over the same routes to establish optimum valve lead which was progressively increased from nil to ½in. It was found that ⅜in lead gave the best results, and during November 1913 further tests took place with this in conjunction with exhaust clearance values mf ¹⁄₁₆in, ⅛in, and ³⁄₁₆in. (The last 4-6-0, No 1525, had originally been turned out new in March 1909 with 'increased' exhaust clearance, although the original design settings have not been established.)

On account of World War 1 the new Dynamometer Car saw no use at all for precisely four years, but some time before hostilities ceased it emerged on 21 July 1918, again behind No 1506, when the latter worked from Manchester to Blackpool and back, with George Hughes himself in attendance. The main purpose of the exercise was to provide data for proposed alterations to schedules, but at the same time it was roughly computed that coal consumption was of the order of 7lb/DBHP hr.

Always very heavy on maintenance, there were occasions when almost the entire class could be found in works. By this time the 4-6-0s were in very poor condition. No 1519 in particular was returning the collosal coal consumption for a passenger engine of 100lb per mile between Southport and York. There was surely some irony in the fact that the 60 leading passenger engines on the line, the 4-4-2s and 4-6-0s, were all still running with saturated boilers in 1918 although Horwich had devoted so much energy to experimental work on superheaters. Some of the later-built 4-4-2s had originally been given a form of smokebox steam drier, but when these engines were given new boilers during 1909-18 the opportunity was not taken to give them true superheaters.

At least one 4-6-0 was experimentally fitted with a different form of smokebox steam drier in 1909. In this each of the two 5½in bore branch pipes split into 16 1⅜in OD copper tubes. These passed back and forth and around the inside of the smokebox wrapper plate, which as in all large-boilered LYR engines was lagged, without in any way obstructing the firetubes, unlike the not entirely dissimilar and contemporary Phoenix arrangement. It is doubtful if this installation achieved the extra 95°F accredited to the Aspinall steam driers on the 4-4-2s. Late in 1913 No 1509 was fitted with a Field tube superheater whose 38 co-axial elements were inserted into a corresponding number of 2¼in firetubes, but this was removed after about two years.

It said a great deal for the indifferent performance of the non-superheated 4-6-0s that the six engines stationed at the LYR's No 1 shed, Newton Heath were displaced elsewhere in 1911, by the arrival of several new superheated 2-4-2 tanks! Serious thoughts of superheating the 4-6-0s in a more conventional manner went back to late 1914 at least, but were delayed by the war. At last in 1916 Horwich prepared drawings for a superheated 4-6-0 boiler which was to incorporate Hughes' ultimate form of superheater with top and bottom headers, with 28 4¾in flues arranged in two vertical banks as newly developed on the large-boilered 0-8-0 goods engines. However, towards the end of the war, 20 of the latter were turned out with saturated boilers for economy reasons. Similarly, although five of the new boilers were ordered for the 4-6-0s in January 1918, these were actually built without superheaters.

In any case to exploit superheated steam the original slide valve cylinders would have been quite inadequate, and indeed when E. S. Cox entered Horwich Drawing Office in February 1919 he discovered that drawings were well advanced for a completely new 4-6-0 chassis with piston valve cylinders having outside steam pipes and served by long travel Walschaerts valve gear. This time the *inside* valves were driven indirectly by rockers, and although maximum travel in full gear was 6⅜in, Cox later expressed his disappointment at the adoption of a valve lap of only 1³⁄₁₆in, after the 1½in lap of the four superheater 4-4-0 rebuilds of 1909. A new cab with side windows was to be provided and the footplate appeared to abound in reverse curves in a most distinctive and attractive fashion.

By the end of 1919 most of the 4-6-0s were laid up awaiting extensive repairs and the first superheater conversion, No 1522, was completed towards the end of October 1920. On 12 November it made a test run out of Hellifield with 293¾ tons to the accompaniment of alternately light and heavy exhaust beats. On 5 December another test run was made from Manchester to Blackpool with 385 tons, whence a 34 per cent improvement in fuel economy, or 4.4lb/DBHP hr, was calculated compared to No 1506's July 1918 *datum*. Details were published in considerable detail in *The Engineer* for 15 April 1921, from which a remarkable disparity was discernible between the outward and return runs. The down run (average 745DBHP) involved several short but severe ascents and was achieved at an average speed of 40.7mph, but at a cost of no less than 75.4lb of coal per mile, and 4.941lb/DBHP hr. The easier return, at 41.6mph, and 685DBHP average consumed only 55lb per mile, and 3.92lb/DBHP hr.

A week or so later No 1522 hauled nine saloons aggregating 333 tons (with the Dynamometer Car) containing LYR 'top brass', including the CME and General Manager from Manchester to Blackpool and happily gained seven minutes on the booked time. Fourteen more 'conversions' rapidly followed up to June 1921, but these likewise were virtually new engines incorporating new frames, boilers and cylinders. Even new numberplates were cast bearing the date 1921. Originally the renewal of all 20 of the original 4-6-0s had been sanctioned in January 1920, together with 15 new engines to the modernised design, but in reality five of the former never were rebuilt. This would seem to have been on account of the still new 1918 non-superheated boilers finding their way onto those engines whose slide-valve cylinders were in the best condition.

Under a new locomotive classification system introduced in early 1920 the Hughes 4-6-0s became Class 8 (the Aspinall 4-4-2s being Class 7). In theory the superheater 4-6-0s should have become Class 9, but no such distinction was ever made.

Extensive tests were carried out with the conversions in order to determine optimum blastpipe diameter and pitch. This culminated in No 1525 hauling the Dynamometer Car and 75 waggons, totalling 1205 tons, between Crofton Junction and Mytholmroyd in October 1921. Two months later No 1519 worked between Crewe and Carlisle with the less sophisticated LNWR Whale test vehicle.

This was the first occasion upon which a Hughes 4-6-0 had reached the Border City, but these engines were already no strangers to stretches of the West Coast main line. Before 1914 in their original non-superheated condition, they had occasionally appeared between Preston and Oxenholme on LYR Manchester-Windermere through passenger services. Towards the end of World War 1 on rare occasions they ventured as far south as Stafford working between Merseyside and Bushbury on American Troop Specials. Although the merger between the LNWR and LYR did not formally take effect until January 1922, 50 years after such had first seriously been mooted, for some time the two concerns had moved closer together, relations being extremely cordial. The forthcoming marriage was discussed in April 1921 and only four months later the last 'conversion', No 1519, was regularly working the LNWR 06.45 Euston-Windermere train between Crewe and Preston, and between Crewe and Fleetwood, soon to be joined by brand new 4-6-0s in the 1649 series which had just begun to emerge from Horwich that month. The appearance of the Hughes 4-6-0s south of Crewe was short lived, and after about 1926 was normally confined to football specials and excursions.

During 1922 a few Hughes 4-6-0s were drafted to Crewe to work north to Carlisle, and were given eight-wheeled tenders (off 0-8-0s) for the purpose. These were more in keeping with the proportions of the engines than their diminutive standard six-wheelers. Meanwhile a new six-wheeled tender, having the standard LNWR capacity of 3,000gal, was designed late in 1922 but did not appear until early LMS days. The numberplates of those engines completed after the LNWR/LYR merger were inscribed LNWR in place of LYR, but neither faction mutually renumbered its engines in view of the approaching much greater amalgamation.

The Hughes 4-6-0s were somewhat unexpectedly thrust into a position of some prominence on account of George Hughes himself being successively appointed CME of the 'Greater LNWR' in 1922, and of the LMSR upon the latter's formation in 1923. No 1662, soon renumbered as LMS No 10433, was popularly regarded as 'the first LMS locomotive', because it entered traffic on 1 January 1923, and it initially bore the short lived inscription LM&SR on the tender. This and succeeding engines soon acquired the handsome new 3,000gal tenders of which about 40 were built. During 1926 several Hughes 4-6-0s were temporarily converted to oil burning.

The newly formed LMS very early gave serious thought to electrifying the West Coast main line, and during the latter half of 1923 in order to provide some basic data some tests took place with pairs of Hughes 4-6-0s on trains of up to 640 tons between Crewe and Carlisle, of which fortunately some photographic record still exists.

Tests still continued with the Hughes 4-6-0s in their own right well into 1924, in order to determine optimum valve proportions by varying the lap, lead and exhaust clearance. No 1656 was the guinea pig and by increasing the lap from 1$\frac{3}{16}$in to 1$\frac{3}{8}$in the engine could work at low speeds with full regulator and at cut-offs as short as 20 per cent. A slightly longer lap of 1$\frac{7}{16}$in was subsequently applied to the final 20 4-6-0s, which had originally been authorised as tank locomotives, the last of which entered traffic in February 1925.

Such had been the close-knit nature of the former Lancashire &

Yorkshire Railway system, that latterly 70 per cent of its passenger mileage was worked by 2-4-2 radial tank engines. No fewer than 330 of these were built at Horwich between 1889 and 1911, the final 20 with superheaters, with which some earlier engines were later rebuilt. There were no fewer than 16 distinct variants, but attempts in 1903-4 to extrapolate these into a larger 2-6-2T, also with inside cylinders, were particularly unsuccessful. Allegedly inspired by the majestic Whitelegg 4-6-4Ts built for the Glasgow & South Western Railway in 1922, Hughes contemplated a 'Baltic' tank version of his own four-cylinder 4-6-0.

Originally no fewer than 60 of the new 4-6-4Ts were envisaged by the newly formed LMS, and orders for 40 of these were placed on Crewe Works. A pilot batch of 10 was built at Horwich Works in early 1924, but shortly *before* the first of these had even made its trial trip on 19 March, it had been decided to turn out succeeding batches as 4-6-0 tender locomotives instead. Although of quite magnificent appearance, especially those accorded the full red passenger livery, it proved difficult to find suitable duties for the 10 4-6-4Ts built on account of their not inconsiderable weight (100 tons) and limited fuel and water supplies. Examples were tried on the Manchester-Buxton and St Pancras-Bedford services, but the engines drifted back to their native Central Division to end their short lives before being withdrawn from service during 1938-1941. Even so the 4-6-4Ts actually lasted longer than many of the 4-6-0s, but such had been their limited usefulness that about 1931 it was actually contemplated rebuilding them as tender locomotives.

Tests conducted in the Manchester area in July 1930 between a Hughes 4-6-4T and a standard Fowler two-cylinder 2-6-4T showed that the smaller engine could perform the same work on 19 per cent less fuel. Furthermore, the use of four cylinders in a tank locomotive was an expensive, and all but unique luxury in British practice.

Although orders for the additional 4-6-4Ts had been cancelled, materials had been assembled for at least 20, and so these were turned out from Horwich as 4-6-0 tender engines by cutting back the main frames. There were detailed differences from the earlier 4-6-0s in that the main frames were noticeably more robust at the front end, and the bogie wheelbase was increased from 6ft 6in to 7ft 0in. The grate area was increased from 27 to 29.6sq ft by reducing the width of the firebox foundation ring from 4in to 3in. These boilers (and those of the 4-6-4Ts) were class RS, as against class KS of the earlier engines. This distinction merely reflected the position of the expansion bracket on the firebox sides. There were never any spare boilers, originally there were 50 KS and 30 RS boilers (plus five non-superheated class K, soon scrapped). Later six KS boilers were converted to RS, whilst some other KS boilers also got the larger grates in the course of heavy repairs, a factor which does not appear to have influenced performance on the road.

The last 20 4-6-0s (Nos 10455-10474) were sent new to Carlisle Upperby, where they remained until 1932-35, occasionally working *north* to Glasgow Central, despite their maximum height of 13ft 5in. With their smaller coupled wheels, larger diameter boilers, and generally more up to date design, the Hughes 4-6-0s should have put the 'Claughtons' in the shade north of Crewe. Their more comfortable cabs were much appreciated, but the higher pitch of the firehole made them more difficult to fire. In reality the Hughes 4-6-0s barely measured up to the 'Claughtons' and suffered from similar ills for slightly different reasons.

Long non-stop runs had been unknown on the old LYR and the lubrication arrangements on the 4-6-0s were simply not up to the long hard slogs over the Westmorland fells. Coupled axle journals on the Class 8 measured 8½in by 9in as against 8¼in by 9¾in in the 'Claughton', axleloads being similar at about 20 tons. Whereas in the LNWR 'Princes' it was the leading, and in the 'Claughtons' the trailing axleboxes which were most prone to heating, in the Hughes 4-6-0s the *intermediate* boxes were most at risk. A survey in 1930 showed that the Hughes 4-6-0s 'enjoyed' the highest incidence of hot boxes of any major LMS passenger design, with on average one casualty per 38,600 miles run compared to 133,330 miles by the new 'Royal Scots'.

Steaming, as in the 'Claughtons', could be erratic due to the ingress of air into the built up smokebox, which rested upon a fabricated saddle. The breeches pipes, which conducted the exhaust steam to the blastpipe nozzle, were each secured to the base of the smokebox by only four studs. With steam shut off smokebox char could become drawn into the cylinders with unpleasant results.

As in the 'Claughtons' also, performance and efficiency would noticeably fall as mileage advanced since last shopping, again due to piston valve design. Horwich piston valves incorporated a Hughes-patented compression release mechanism within their heads which each incorporated several small steel balls. These wore into irregular shapes over a period of time resulting in very

severe wastage of steam. In the 1930s these were replaced on several engines by new-style piston valves with six narrow rings. Surprisingly this does *not* appear to have significantly reduced the coal consumption of the class, according to data presented graphically by E. S. Cox in 1946.

No positive details appear to survive concerning the comparative trials between 'Claughton' No 192 and superheated Hughes Class 8 No 1521 on the LYR between Manchester and Blackpool in the Autumn of 1921, although Cox avers that the latter did now show up with particular distinction on its home ground. The only straight comparison of which we have record was the Preston-Carlisle trials of May 1925, which also involved an ex-LNW 'Prince' and the inevitable Derby Compound. No 10460 had the advantage over No 1521 of longer lap valves and a larger grate, but was notably heavier on coal than the 'Claughton'. On the credit side the Horwich engine developed a greater DBHP at a higher speed by charging Shap bank at full power, whereas the 'Claughton' had only been opened out on the final portion of the climb, by which time its speed had fallen appreciably.

Locomotive trials Preston-Carlisle, May 1925

	MR Compound 4-4-0 No 1065	LNWR 'Prince' 4-6-0 No 90	LNWR 'Claughton' 4-6-0 No 30		LYR-type 4-6-0 No 10460	
Mileage out of shops	28,063	7,500	22,977		20,788	
Train weight, tons	350	350	350	400	350	400
Maximum DBHP	965	875	975	1000	1075	1075
Speed at max DBHP	49	40	32	31	44	44
Coal consumption:						
lb/DBHP hr	4.25	5.05	4.78	4.75	5.07	5.13
lb/mile	43.4	48.3	42.4	52.7	51.3	58.1

It was a fact that the ultimate LYR 4-6-0 passenger and 0-8-0 heavy freight designs were heavier on coal (per mile) than their LNWR counterparts, the 'Claughton' and 'G2'. Three Hughes 4-6-0s, Nos 10432-4, were fitted with the Dabeg feedwater heater and pump, and the first named was tested on Club trains between Manchester and Blackpool in October 1927. For comparative purposes alternate runs were made with the normal live steam injector, and then the Dabeg apparatus in operation:

	Live steam injector	Dabeg FWH	Saving
Coal consumption:			
lb/DBHP hr	4.15	3.68	11.3%
lb/mile	55.7	44.9	19.4%

Although the Dabeg apparatus undoubtedly wrought a considerable economy in fuel consumption, in terms of lb/DBHP hr this cannot have been so good as above, for a defect was inadvertently discovered in the mechanism of the No 1 Dynamometer car, which resulted in enhanced values for apparent drawbar thermal efficiency, the error being as high as 30 per cent! To what extent this defect had influenced the results of earlier LMS locomotive tests is problematical, but in the light of this they must remain suspect, being valid more in comparative rather than absolute terms.

Hughes had been thwarted in his attempts during 1923-1924 to develop his 4-6-0 into a wide firebox 4-6-2, and a 2-8-2 heavy freight counterpart, and he had retired prematurely and somewhat abruptly with effect from the end of September 1925. This would appear to have arisen from his weariness at the three cornered conflict between himself as CME (ex-LYR and English), the Chief Civil Engineer, E. C. Trench (ex-LNWR and Irish), and the Chief of Motive Power, J. E. Anderson (ex-Midland and a Scot).

Below: Power curves for LMS Power Class 5 4-6-0s (LNWR and LYR) on 400 ton trains, Preston-Carlisle, 1925.

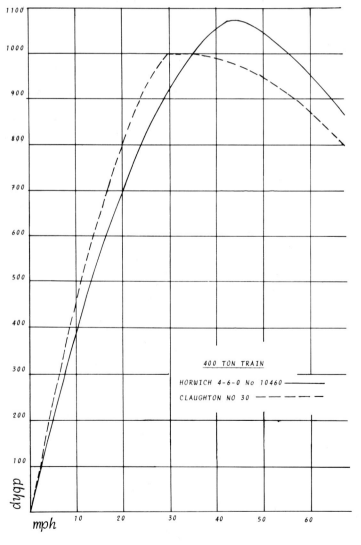

400 TON TRAIN

HORWICH 4-6-0 No 10460 ————

CLAUGHTON NO 30 — — — — —

The latter was an advocate of the Derby small engine policy, and his strong opinions conflicted with those of the CME, whose attempts to produce powerful new locomotives had also found little favour with Trench.

Hughes' successor, Sir Henry Fowler, an ex-Midland man, immediately sought to persevere with the 4-6-2 and 2-8-2 schemes but re-vamped as four-cylinder compounds. All three major drawing offices deliberately seem to have been brought together to produce a joint effort under the overall co-ordination of Horwich, which also concentrated on the valve gear. Derby worked on the boiler, ostensibly for the 2-8-2.* Crewe produced drawings for the cylinders, and on 1 March 1926 received an order to build five compound 4-6-2s.

Fabrication had already commenced when a complete halt was called in early October, following the appearance on trial of the brand new GWR four-cylinder 4-6-0 No 5000 *Launceston Castle* at Euston. At whose behest this trial was made is not entirely clear, but it certainly was not that of the CME who, as E. S. Cox has pointed out in *Locomotive Panorama* Volume 1 (Ian Allan Ltd, 1965), was far from being the god-like figure of popular imagination.

In order to provide some useful data Horwich got out a scheme in October 1925 to rebuild a Hughes 4-6-0 as a compound. The original two sets of valve gear were to be retained, ie without provision for independent HP and LP cut-offs, but the starting valve arrangements, whereby live steam could be admitted to the LP cylinders when in full gear, was based on Hughes' four-cylinder compound 0-8-0s of 1906-7. No 10456 was selected for rebuilding, thereby acquiring new 22in by 26in inside LP cylinders, but the only detectable superficial difference was the provision of noticeably wider outside steampipe casings.

Rather strangely No 10456 was only tested against another otherwise similar 4-6-0 between Preston and Carlisle as late as July 1930. These tests were of academic interest as being the only instance in British practice of which there is record, of the evaluation of a *superheated* compound *with conventional boiler*. The fuel savings achieved were only moderate being 9.8 per cent on a lb/mile basis, and only 8.0 per cent in terms of lb/DBHP hr. The report on the tests made the following observations:

(1) The moderate nominal boiler pressure of 180lb in practice amounted to 10-12lb less.
(2) There was a great disparity in mileage run since last shopping, Compound No 10456 having accrued no less than 43,002 miles,

as compared to only 3,878 miles by Simple No 10464. It was suggested that had both been tested at 20,000 miles the former would have shown up better due to lower steam loss through wear.
(3) The expansive possibilities were actually less for steam exhausting from 16in into 22in bore cylinders than compared to four 16½in simple cylinders.
(4) The greater economy of the Compound was due to the lower temperature range in each cylinder, with consequent reduced heat loss and leakage.

No 10456 would also have shown a much greater efficiency if it had been tested when newly converted in 1926. Data presented by E. S. Cox 20 years later showed that the average annual coal consumption per mile of this engine climbed steadily from 50lb in 1928 to 64lb in 1934, by which time it slightly exceeded the 59-61lb average of the remainder of the class over the period 1928-1938. Thus by 1930 its relative superiority would have appreciably declined, but by all accounts it was a popular locomotive spending most of its obscure life working between Crewe and Carlisle.

The conversion of No 10456 to compound working and the production of the familiar LMS 'Crab' 2-6-0 both in 1926 marked the effective end of Horwich's influence in locomotive design. The 2-6-0 was characterised by large and steeply inclined outside cylinders which were necessitated by Hughes' insistence on the employment of a moderate boiler pressure no greater than 180lb. Hughes was nothing if not practical and under-lying this firm instruction was the fact that firebox stay life in Horwich boilers was short due to poor water circulation. Some vestige of autonomy must have lingered on in Lancashire, however, for clearly in response to Crewe reboiling the 'Claughtons' Horwich in August 1928 proposed rebuilding the Hughes 4-6-0s with new 200lb pressure boilers. The ample diameter of the original boilers was to be retained in conjunction with a sloping firebox throatplate, as in the 'Royal Scot' and G9½S boilers, which would have reduced tube length by 19in to 13ft 1in. In the initial scheme the original grate area of 29.6sq ft was to remain, but when the boiler was subsequently developed in some detail on the drawing board this cardinal dimension was increased to 31.6sq ft, which should have conferred enhanced potential.

Somewhat in keeping with this sentiment a chimney some 3in shorter was to be fitted, reposing on a built up smokebox.

* The 2-8-2 at last had Anderson's backing to avoid double-heading on the Toten-Brent coal trains, for which Derby had outlined a succession of powerful 0-8-0 and 2-8-0 proposals during the 1903-1920 period.

Below: 20 years later, final series Hughes superheated 4-6-0 with 3,000gal tender carrying proposed 200lb boiler (1928).

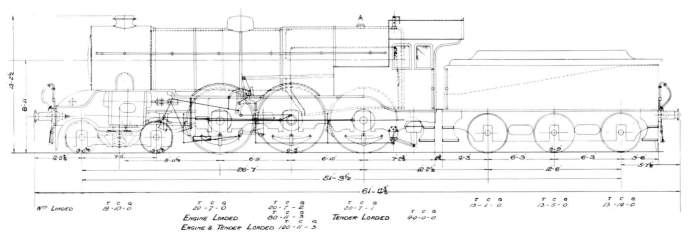

Cylinder diameter was to be reduced from 16½in to 15¾in which would have effectively improved the valve proportions. The proposed boiler was not put into production, but from 1930 17 4-6-0s received new cylinders having this reduced bore. As these did not include any of the final 20 engines (and only one 4-6-4T) this may well have reflected some weakness in the front end frame design of the earlier 4-6-0s. In this regard it is no doubt significant that, from available photographic evidence, the Hughes 4-6-0s whose cabsides were inscribed in 1927 with a prominent letter S, denoting first class mechanical condition suited to top link duties, were all members of the final series originally laid down as 4-6-4Ts. Six engines thus known to have been so designated were Nos. 10455/7/60/7/9/72. This said, as a group the final series enjoyed the shortest working lives of any, with only two still running after early 1937, when a halt was called on scrapping the surviving Hughes 4-6-0s which were overhauled and refurbished.

By 1930 replacement boilers were becoming due and it was proposed that these should be similar to the existing type, but should incorporate conventional 24-element 3-row Schmidt superheaters, as in the proposed 1928 boilers. None were actually built and when Stanier took over as CME in 1932 he initially proposed a vast reboilering programme of existing engines with new standard taper boilers. The 70 4-6-0s and 10 4-6-4Ts were to receive a pattern similar to that fitted to the early 5X 'Jubilee' 4-6-0s. This whole plan was quickly rescinded in favour of a ruthless scrap and build programme and in July 1933 it was decreed that all Horwich 4-6-0s should be condemned upon falling due for new boilers. The first withdrawals soon followed and all would have gone by the end of the 1930s, but for the war. (A proposal to fit their still fairly new 3,000gal tenders to Aspinall 0-6-0s does not appear to have been put into effect.) Nevertheless those 4-6-0s which survived a major visit to works and were given

a repaint before 1940 were accorded the red livery. No fewer than 10 engines, including one conversion (old No 1518) were inherited by British Railways in 1948 but were quickly scrapped, with the exception of the first (and only surviving) example of the final batch, No 10455. This engine made a final valedictory run from Blackpool to York on 1 July 1951 before being condemned a few months later (see Appendix 3).

Unlike the 'Claughtons' the Hughes 4-6-0s appear to have kept almost entirely clear of accidents, and would seem to have been involved in none that resulted in the deaths of passengers. Only one, which involved unrebuilt No 1512 running light engine near Preston in November 1924, fatally injured its crew. In retrospect the super-heated Hughes 4-6-0s could be said to be one of that select band of locomotive 'near misses'. It is a curious fact, however, that as far as the British Isles was concerned, only Swindon seemed to succeed in building a really successful four-cylinder 4-6-0.

LYR 4-6-0 allocations

	1908-9 (when new)	31 December 1921
Newton Heath (No 1)	1513-8 (6)	1517-8 (2)
Low Moor (No 2)	1506-10, 1524 (6)	1516, 1524-5, 1654 (4)
Southport (No 17)	1511-2, 1523 (3)	1506, 1511-2 (3)
Sandhills (Bank Hall) (No 18)	1525 (1)	1507, 1509-10, 1523, 1653 (5)
Fleetwood (No 30)		1652, 1656 (2)
Blackpool (Talbot Road) (No 31)		1519 (1)
Blackpool (Central) (No 32)	1519-1522 (4)	1508, 1513-5, 1520-2, 1649-51, 1655, 1657 (12)

The Hughes 4-6-0s

Left: Newly built, LYR 4-6-0 No 1511 is seen at York. Note the original narrow chimney, and bogie brakes. *Real Photographs*

Top: Double-heading was comparatively rare on the LYR. However, during July 1913 4-6-0s Nos 1514 and 1525 were deputed to haul the LNWR Royal Train. Both were specially provided with eight-wheeled tenders more in keeping with their proportions, and are here seen at Rainford Halt.
Courtesy, National Railway Museum, York

Above: No 1515 again, somewhat earlier in its career, heads a Manchester-Blackpool express on the West Coast main line just south of Preston. *Rixon Bucknall Collection*

Above right: In somewhat begrimed condition No 1515 displays the later condition of the class with wider chimney and bogie brakes removed. Note the very light proportions of the coupling rods and unusual use of four-bar crossheads for outside cylinders. No 1515 was never rebuilt. *Rixon Bucknall Collection*

Right: No 1514 alone hauls the Royal Train during the royal visit to Lancashire in July 1913. The engine is coupled to an eight-wheeled tender.

Top left: Hughes 4–6–0 No 1521 photographed in somewhat woe-begone condition in February 1920. There is no evidence that any of this class ever ran in traffic with GCR-type 4,000gal tenders from ROD 2-8-0s, of which a number operated on the LYR around this time. (Horwich referred to these tenders as NB tenders.) No 1521 emerged completely renewed a year later. *Courtesy, National Railway Museum, York*

Above left: LYR No 1514 still in LYR livery, seen with its LMS number 10406, applied in small numerals. *Ian Allan Library*

Left: Hughes 4–6–0 No 10431 leaves York with a light three-coach train, passing the old LYR locomotive shed. *LPC*

Above: Hughes 4–6–0 No 1662 poses at the head of a rake of LYR corridor stock early in 1923. *Ian Allan Library*

Right: A Hughes 4–6–0 with small tender seen on duty on the West Coast main line. No 10436 takes water at Dillicar troughs with an Edinburgh-Liverpool train. *H. Gordon Tidey*

Above: The first photograph of a superheated Hughes 4–6–0. No 1522 undergoes a steaming test at Horwich on 22 October 1920. Not only were the frames, boiler, cylinders and cab new, but even the coupled wheel centres, whose crankpins were now set at a 13in throw, rather than the 11in of the original engines. Probably the tender, if little else, survived from the original No 1522! *Courtesy, National Railway Museum, York*

Above right: LYR No 1649, the first of the superheater 4–6–0s to be built new to the 'rebuilt' design, and one of the very few to bear the full inscription Lancashire & Yorkshire on the tender.

Below right: 4–6–0 No 1675, completed in July 1923, theoretically the highest numbered locomotive in LYR capital stock and last to receive a cast number plate, seen in dull grey livery when new.

100

Above: 4-6-0 No 1664, one of a handful of Horwich 4-6-0s and
0-8-0s outshopped in early 1923 bearing the rare insignia
LM&SR.

This picture: Another rebuild, No 1518, awaits departure from
York with a Newcastle-Liverpool express.
Rixon Bucknall Collection

No 10430, originally LNWR-built in 1922, in LMS red livery, with 3,000gal tender.
Real Photographs

Above: The Hughes superheated Class 8 was surely the most modern looking British 4-6-0 in 1923. Here brand new No 1670, completed in May 1923, displays the new-type 3,000gal tender specially designed for service on the Western Division. Interestingly, although the Lancashire & Yorkshire Railway had ceased to exist as such almost 18 months previously and the engine was lettered LMS, the livery style is pure LYR. The cast number plates (inscribed LMS) were very short-lived, for the engine soon became LMS No 10441.
Courtesy, National Railway Museum, York

Above right: During late 1920-1921 Hughes 4-6-0s worked very heavy test trains between Manchester and Blackpool, but their activities soon extended to the West Coast main line. Here newly built No 1657 with eight-wheeled tender is seen with the LYR Dynamometer Car and train on 13 June 1922 at an unrecorded location on the LNWR.
Courtesy, National Railway Museum, York

Right: The final engine of the original batch of 20, No 1525 was provided with modified valve events and is here seen on test with an indicator shelter attached.

Above left: Only two Hughes 4-6-0s, Nos 10447 and 10474, were turned out new in red livery, but most if not all acquired it in due course. So altered No 10464 of the final series is seen at Crewe. Although the latter were most noticeably different at the front end, their cabs, boilers, and valve gear also differed in detail from the earlier engines. *Real Photographs*

Left: The 10 4-6-4T engines, and the final 20 4-6-0s Nos 10455-10474, originally laid down as such, initially entered traffic in dull dark grey paint. No 10458 with diminutive cabside numerals is seen at Crewe.

Above: First of the final series, and destined to be the last survivor, in its prime in red livery No 10455 sports the special S on its cabside.

Above right: The last Hughes 4-6-0 built, No 10474, equipped for oil burning in 1926.

Right: No 10458 heads the 10.5am Glasgow-Euston, lost in a cloud of spray over Dillicar troughs on 18 June 1928. *L. J. Thompson*

Hughes 4–6–0s on the Central Division

Above: Several years later in May 1936 No 10423 works a semi-fast over Lea Road troughs near Preston. Note the later style smokebox door (introduced on the 4–6–4Ts) and 'blisters' on the front cover plate. The latter modification accompanied the provision of improved piston valves during the 1930s. Compression release valves are now fitted on the cylinder covers. *E. R. Wethersett*

Below: The most enduring of the Hughes 4–6–0s, originally built as LYR No 1516 in 1908 and 'renewed' in 1921, seen still going strong in September 1947 as LMS No 10412 at Manchester Victoria. It was withdrawn from service in February 1949 with over one million miles (in theory at least) to its credit. *P. Ward*

Bottom: One of the longest lived Hughes 4–6–0s was No 10442 of May 1923, condemned in August 1950 after having covered 779,401 miles. Seen at Blackpool Shed in September 1948. The tender is that originally attached to Hughes saturated 4–6–0 No 1518 built in 1908. *J. P. Wilson*

Right: No 10448, with 3,000gal tender, at Blackpool shed, September 1948. *J. P. Wilson*

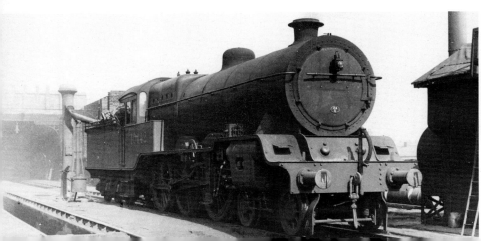

Right: The last survivor, BR No 50455 awaits departure from Blackpool Central on 1 July 1951 with the Stephenson Locomotive Society/Manchester Locomotive Society Blackpool–York special.
E. J. M. Hunt

Below: The only Hughes 4–6–0 to be fully repainted in BR mixed traffic (ie LNW) livery, No 50455 is seen at Manchester Victoria, en route for York for the last time.
Ian Allan Library

Above: The solitary compound 4-6-0 No 10456, converted for experimental purposes when only two years old and seen at Carlisle Upperby shed in September 1934, about 18 months before withdrawal. *W. Leslie Good*

Left: In an attempt to reduce coal consumption, three Hughes 4-6-0s allocated to the Central Division in 1925 were equipped with Dabeg feedwater heaters with satisfactory results. Here is No 10433 so fitted. *Real Photographs*

Below left: No 10468 was fitted c1928 with Kylala draughting arrangements. This was discernible visually by a noticeably wider chimney, and audibly by a distinctly hollow exhaust. The engine still retained these features when photographed in 1934. *W. Leslie Good*

The Hughes 4-6-4Ts

Right: Other than initially entering traffic in dull grey most of the 10 Hughes 4-6-4Ts were painted black throughout their comparatively short lives. This included the prototype, No 11110, seen here at Manchester Victoria in April 1939. *J. P. Wilson*

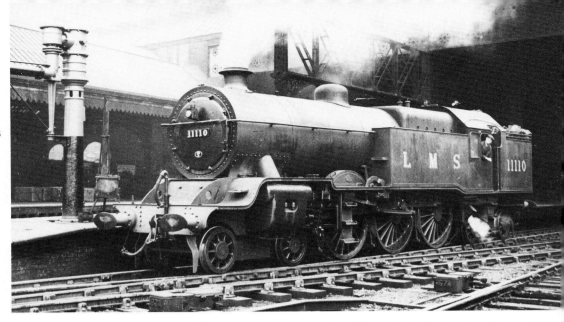

Below right: No 11112 in fully lined out crimson lake livery, so attired for exhibition purposes at the Stockton & Darlington Railway Centenary celebrations in July 1925, at which the final Hughes 4-6-0, No 10474, also appeared painted red.

Below: Very few photographs exist of the Hughes 4-6-4Ts at work outside their native Lancashire, none at all it would appear of them operating on the St Pancras-Bedford services. This rare photograph shows the uniquely numbered 11111 (then recently repainted red) at Combs near Chapel-en-le-Frith on a Manchester-Buxton train in May 1929.
S. T. Cowan Collection, Courtesy, National Railway Museum, York

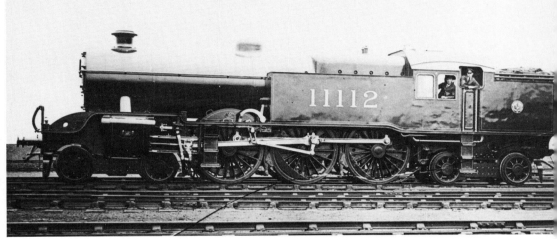

Right: The Whale Dynamometer Car built by the LNWR at Wolverton in 1908. Originally un-numbered it became LMS No 45051 in 1933, and was designated LMS No 2 Dynamometer Car. Used sporadically for locomotive testing until 1939, it was converted for use with flange force testing experiments in 1946 and was finally condemned in August 1968.
Courtesy, National Railway Museum, York

Below right: Hughes Dynamometer Car built by the LYR at Newton Heath in 1912. Later became LMS No 1 Dynamometer Car, being extensively modified c1929. Originally LYR No 293 it became LMS No 10874, being renumbered to 45050 in 1933 and BR No M45050. It last functioned in August 1967 and is now preserved at the Midland Railway Centre, Butterley.
Courtesy, National Railway Museum, York

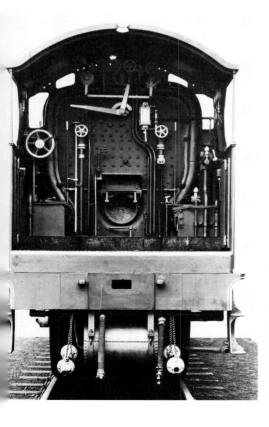

Cab Views of West Coast 4-Cylinder 4-6-0s

Left: An interesting comparison of the cab layouts of LNWR No 2222 (left) and LYR No 1522 (right). In the tradition of the Aspinall 4-4-2s introduced in 1899 the Horwich 4-6-0s were designed to be driven sitting down. Such enlightenment was not apparent on the 'Claughtons', which with typical Crewe parsimony were provided with only one gauge glass. Whilst North Western drivers liked the greater comfort and thoughtful layout of the Hughes 4-6-0 cabs, their firemen did not appreciate the higher pitch of the firehole.
Courtesy, National Railway Museum, York

10
From 4-4-2 to 4-6-2 at St Rollox

Writing in *Cassier's Magazine* for March 1910, John F. McIntosh, Locomotive Superintendent of the Caledonian Railway, emphatically claimed that the 4-4-2 type 'had not been a conspicuous success anywhere'. We now know that nearly five years earlier he had himself sought and obtained sanction to build five such locomotives, a plan which was subsequently abandoned. Indeed, more than 70 years later it is possible to trace with some accuracy the course of locomotive development at St Rollox from 1896 to 1923, a story which includes some non-existent missing links which progressed no further than the drawing board. On few other British railways did locomotives, and proposed locomotives, increase so rapidly in size and theoretical power over such a relatively short period, as on the Caledonian Railway around the turn of the century.

In January 1896 McIntosh had produced his classic 4-4-0 CR No 721 *Dunalastair*. At the time this was much acclaimed on account of the size of its boiler, which was actually only 3in greater at 4ft 9in than the corresponding dimension on McIntosh's predecessor John Lambie's 4-4-0s. It was nonetheless a crucial step, and the following year, 1897, boiler pressure and heating surface were increased to produce the 'Dunalastair II'. In 1899 appeared the so-called 'Dunalastair III' in which grate area was increased from 20.6 to 22sq ft to match the increase in power, and adhesive weight had risen by 3½ tons in but three years.

Such progressive increases could barely keep pace with contemporary train weights and speeds and in 1901 McIntosh began to look beyond the 4-4-0, initially at the 4-4-2. In September 1901 when his initial Atlantic proposal was outlined only 31 4-4-2s were at work in the British Isles, with 11 on the GNR and 20 on the LYR. These aggregated only 32 and 35 tons on the coupled wheels respectively, whereas McIntosh's proposal boasted no less than 37 tons which was not equalled by any contemporary 4-4-0.

By April 1902 the 4-4-2 scheme had been discarded in favour of a dimensionally similar 4-6-0, concerning which there was some debate as to whether coupled wheel diameter should be reduced to 6ft from the standard 6ft 6in in conjunction with 20½in by 26in cylinders. In the event the larger wheel diameter was retained, and a nominal cylinder bore of no less than 21in, as in the recent '600' class 0-8-0s, was specified. Two such engines, CR Nos 49 and 50, made their appearance in the Spring of 1903.

As the writer has previously described in Chapter 5 of *The Scottish 4-6-0 Classes* (Ian Allan, 1976) the new locomotives were not without their attendant problems. Cylinder diameter was soon reduced to 20in, boiler pressure was possibly reduced from 200lb to 175lb and tube length decreased by recessing the smokebox tubeplate further into the boiler barrel. The original hope that banking assistance on Beattock could be avoided was soon forgotten, and certainly no longer feasible following the material reduction in tractive effort.

The big 4-6-0s with their longer and shallower fireboxes required entirely different firing techniques from the more numerous 4-4-0s and their performance undoubtedly suffered as a

Below: J. F. McIntosh's original 4-4-2 proposal of September 1901, subsequently developed into the '49' class 4-6-0 completed in March 1903.

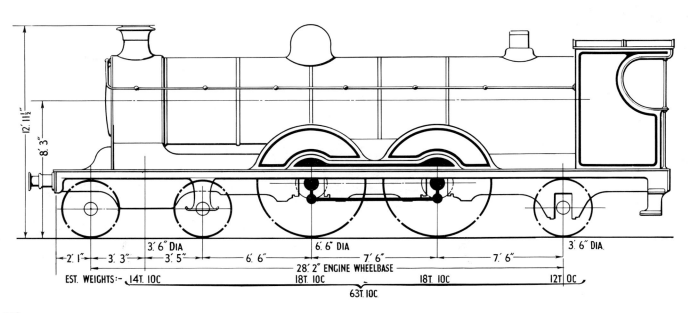

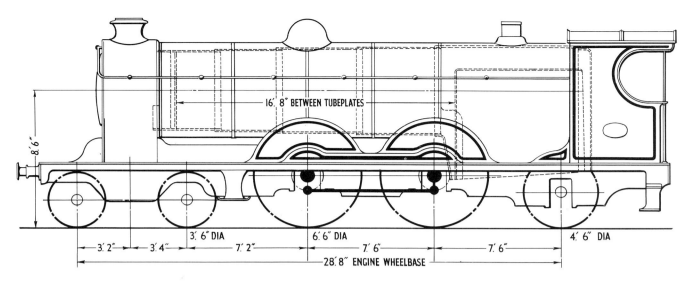

Diagram labels: 16' 8" BETWEEN TUBEPLATES · 8' 6" · 3' 6" DIA · 6' 6" DIA · 4' 6" DIA · 3' 2" · 3' 4" · 7' 2" · 7' 6" · 7' 6" · 28' 8" ENGINE WHEELBASE

Above: McIntosh's inside-cylinder 4–4–2 scheme of 1905 and actually authorised, but superseded by the '903' class 4-6-0s.

direct result. The period 1903-1906 witnessed considerable uncertainty as to relative advantages of the 4-4-2 against the 4-6-0, and on balance the former at the time seemed to come out better, despite its lower adhesive weight, probably because of the greater room available for a deeper firebox and better ashpan arrangement. It is not perhaps insignificant that during 1905 McIntosh once again looked at the 4-4-2, and rumours that the appearance of such on the Caledonian was imminent actually reached the popular railway press.

Also in 1905 compounding was all the rage and in March St Rollox Drawing Office outlined a four-cylinder 4-4-2 compounded on the de Glehn system. This progressed no further on the drawing board than skeletal overall locomotive and valve gear arrangements and was quickly abandoned. Two months later a more conventional inside-cylinder 4-4-2 was put forward, which utilised the compound's boiler.

In November 1905 five inside-cylinder 4-4-2s were authorised by the Caledonian Board 'to work the Edinburgh and Carlisle express trains and down tourist and postal trains between Carlisle, Perth and Aberdeen'. It is thus clear that McIntosh's Atlantic (Mark 3) was intended to work over Beattock as well as the relatively undemanding route between Perth and Aberdeen. In the event it was stillborn and work went ahead on five dimensionally similar 4-6-0s which had been sanctioned simultaneously. As first outlined in September 1905 these were to have had 6ft coupled wheels and an estimated weight of 69½ tons. When they duly appeared in May-June 1906 coupled wheel diameter had been

increased to 6ft 6in and actual weight in working order was 72½ tons.

Thus the celebrated '903' class was born. No 903 itself bore the name *Cardean* and became a legend in its own lifetime, working the up and down 'corridor' with great regularity between Glasgow and Carlisle for a decade. Its resplendent image was somewhat tarnished on the evening of 2 April 1909 near Crawford, where as the result of an apparent crank axle failure, locomotive and train parted company and the latter ground to a halt, derailed but intact. This near disaster has never been fully explained, but the subsequent Board of Trade report put the blame squarely on the design of the crank axle and its mode of manufacture.

Hitherto very much an inside-cylinder man, it is a curious fact that during his last five years in office McIntosh subsequently caused to be outlined several fast six-coupled main line engines with *outside* cylinders. The most impressive of these, and designed in some detail, was a superheated version of the '903' class of striking mien, partly because the boiler was to be raised 3in. The initial scheme was dated February 1911, at which time a start was made on rebuilding the '49' and '903' classes with Schmidt superheaters and piston valves, an operation completed five months later. Regrettably this fine 4-6-0 was not built in this form, although it was later to be revived by McIntosh's successor.

Caledonian Railway 4-4-2/4-6-0 development 1901-1906

	Proposed 4-4-2	'49' class 4-6-0 as built	'49' class 4-6-0 modified	Proposed 4-4-2	'903' class 4-6-0
	1901	*1903*	*1904*	*1905*	*1906*
Cylinders	(I) 20½in × 26in	(I) 21in × 26in	(I) 20in × 26in	(I) 20in × 26in	(I) 20in × 26in
Driving wheel dia	6ft 6in	6ft 6in	6ft 6in	6ft 6in	6ft 6in
Boiler pressure (lb)	180	200	175	200	200
Tube length		17ft 3in	15ft 8in	16ft 8in	16ft 8in
Total evaporative (sq ft)	2,225	2,323	2,032	2,275	2,266
Grate area (sq ft)	26.5	26.0	26.0	26.0	26.0
Adhesion weight (tons)	27.0	55.0	53.5		54.5
Engine weight (tons)	63.5	73.0	70.0	71.0	73.0
Tractive effort (lb)	21,500	25,000	19,900	22,700	22,700

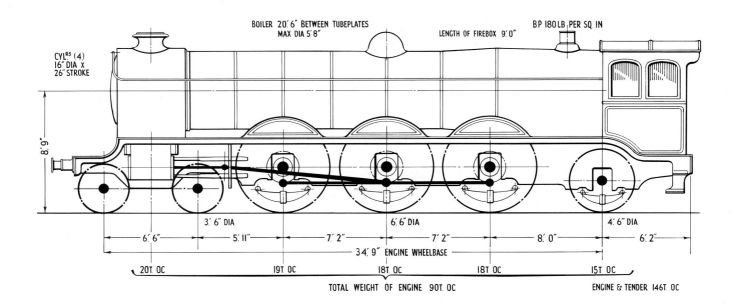

BOILER 20'6" BETWEEN TUBEPLATES
MAX DIA 5'8"

LENGTH OF FIREBOX 9'0"

B.P 180 LB PER SQ IN

CYL^RS (4)
16" DIA x
26" STROKE

8'9"

3'6" DIA   6'6" DIA   4'6" DIA

6'6"   5'11"   7'2"   7'2"   8'0"   6'2"

34'9" ENGINE WHEELBASE

20T OC   19T OC   18T OC   18T OC   15T OC

TOTAL WEIGHT OF ENGINE 90T OC   ENGINE & TENDER 146T OC

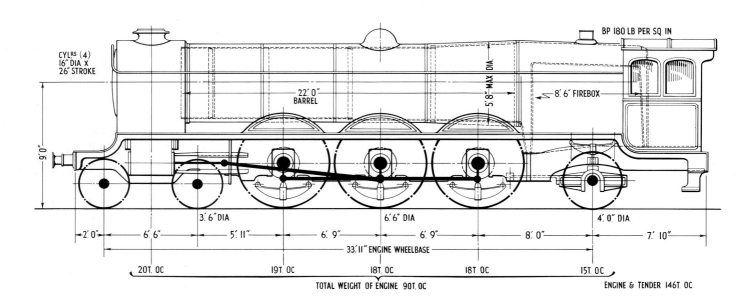

BP 180 LB PER SQ IN

CYL^RS (4)
16" DIA x
26" STROKE

22'0"
BARREL

5'8" MAX DIA

8'6" FIREBOX

9'0"

3'6" DIA   6'6" DIA   4'0" DIA

2'0"   6'6"   5'11"   6'9"   6'9"   8'0"   7'10"

33'11" ENGINE WHEELBASE

20T OC   19T OC   18T OC   18T OC   15T OC

TOTAL WEIGHT OF ENGINE 90T OC   ENGINE & TENDER 146T OC

Above: The proposed four-cylinder Pacifics of October 1913.

Whilst admittedly administering a smaller locomotive fleet McIntosh had consistently managed to keep one jump ahead of Crewe. His first two large-wheeled 4-6-0s had appeared two years before Whale's *Experiment*. McIntosh's superheated 4-4-0 No 139 was an exact contemporary of LNWR No 2663 *George the Fifth*, and all seven 6ft 6in 4-6-0s had been rebuilt with superheaters by the time LNWR No 819 *Prince of Wales* emerged from Crewe. Crewe at last stole a march on St Rollox early in 1913 by producing the four-cylinder 'Claughtons'.

It was surely a move to put St Rollox in the lead again that in his last months in office in the Autumn of 1913 McIntosh had a four-cylinder 4-6-2 drawn out. Dimensionally poor with small semi-wide firebox affording only 37sq ft of grate, this proposal has previously been described elsewhere in several places, but it is not generally known that it was immediately preceded by another 4-6-2 scheme which would have featured an even smaller *narrow*

firebox yielding only 27sq ft of grate. Tube length would have been truly excessive in both schemes and steaming would assuredly have been a very touchy business had either been built.

McIntosh retired early in 1914 and was succeeded by William Pickersgill, late of the Great North of Scotland Railway. Pickersgill made no move to proceed with McIntosh's proposed Pacific, but he did take up the outside-cylinder passenger 4-6-0 proposal, but with the coupled wheel diameter reduced to 6ft 1in, a GN of S standard, and six-wheel in place of bogie tender. The initial diagram for the Directors' approval was dated 14 June 1914, but the outbreak of World War 1 soon afterwards resulted in the six engines subsequently authorised not appearing until 1916-7 as CR Nos 60-65.

Twenty more of these locomotives were subsequently built by the LMS during 1925-6, but their performance was generally unexciting and verged on the sluggish. In later years the one claim to fame of the '60' class was the apparent immunity of the 1¼in thick main frames to cracking. It is thus strange to read in the 24

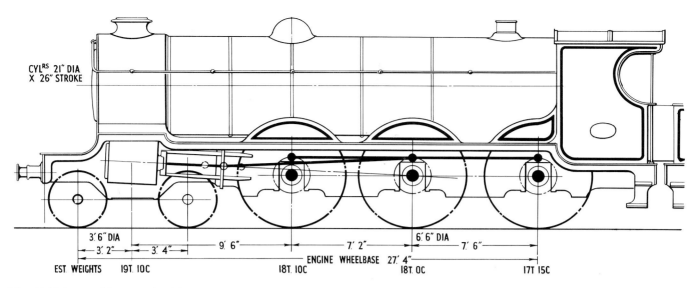

CYL^{RS} 21″ DIA X 26″ STROKE

3′ 6″ DIA   6′ 6″ DIA

3′ 2″   3′ 4″   9′ 6″   7′ 2″   7′ 6″

ENGINE WHEELBASE 27′ 4″

EST. WEIGHTS   19T. 10C   18T. 10C   18T. 0C   17T. 15C

Above: The proposed McIntosh superheated outside-cylinder express passenger 4-6-0 of 1911, subsequently developed by Pickersgill into the indifferent '60' class.

May 1919 issue of *Locomotive News and Railway Notes* that 'the (Caledonian Railway) "60" class have not been a success so far, the chief trouble being the frames, the material of which seems to have been faulty. The first to give was 61 at the end of last July'.

It is interesting to contrast the CR '60' class and LNWR 'Princes'. Both designs were endowed with remarkably similar boiler and cylinder capacity, but the former had outside cylinders and massive main frames, whereas the latter had inside cylinders and very light main frames which were notoriously prone to cracking. Tests conducted between Preston and Carlisle with 350ton trains during 1925-6 appeared to demonstrate a similar level of thermodynamic efficiency, with both returning coal consumptions of the order of 50lb to the mile, and 4.8-5.0lb/DBHP hr.

The CR '60' class and LNWR 'Prince' compared

	CR '60'	LNWR 'Prince'
Cylinders	20½in × 26in	20½in × 26in
Driving Wheel dia	6ft 1in	6ft 3in
Boiler pressure	175lb	175lb
Evaporative HS	1,529sq ft	1,512sq ft
Superheater	258	304
Grate area	25.5	25.0
Adhesive weight	56.0 tons	42.45 tons
Total weight	74.75	66.5
Max DBHP*	840	875
Speed*	47mph	40mph
Coal consumption:		
lb/DBHP hr*	4.84	5.05
lb/mile*	51.55	48.3

* Preston-Carlisle trials 1925-6 350ton trains.

The 'Prince' packed considerably more verve and although weighing 10 per cent less than the St Rollox 4-6-0 it had the potential to develop 15 per cent more maximum DBHP, although this was not made apparent in 1925. The Pickersgill engine for its part demonstrated commendably low maintenance costs, doubtless assisted in part by the high purity of water supplies in Scotland which resulted in low boiler repair costs. Its generally liberal construction must have been the secret however, and taking a Derby Class 2P 4-4-0 as = 100, the Pickersgill '60' class 4-6-0 came out at 117, and the ex-LNWR 'Prince' at no less than 157. These ratios were first quoted by E. S. Cox in 1946.

Mr Cox personally supervised the dynamometer car trials with the first LMS-built '60', No 14630, between Preston and Carlisle in May 1926. In his subsequent report he made the interesting comment that oil consumption on this engine was very high for a two-cylinder locomotive, being on average 61 per cent greater than that of a 'Prince', but lower than that of the four-cylinder 4-6-0s of Crewe and Horwich design.

Although the engines have always been branded as outright failures, no statistics of fuel, water, and oil consumption appear to have survived for Pickersgill's *magnum opus*, his three-cylinder 4-6-0. Four of these engines, numbered 956-959 were completed at St Rollox in the summer of 1921 at a cost of £9,665 apiece. The design was completely out of character as far as Pickersgill was concerned, as he was normally content to adapt and adopt McIntosh's designs to rather poor effect. What inspired Pickersgill to indulge in three-cylinder propulsion may never be known, but it may be significant that the engines were authorised in December 1918, five weeks after Herbert Holcroft had delivered a paper to the Institution of Locomotive Engineers on three-cylinder locomotives and derived valve gears to operate the inside valve.

Holcroft had been granted a patent for a derived valve gear applicable to a three-cylinder locomotive back in 1909. Railways were always notoriously unwilling to pay royalties to other companies, and unaware that Holcroft's patent had in fact already lapsed, St Rollox Drawing Office sought ways of avoiding infringing it during the winter of 1918-1919.

The mastermind of this operation was one George Kerr, a somewhat aristocratic individual, who unlike all his colleagues, including the Chief Draughtsman, drove himself to work in his own motor car, rather than travelling by tram. Kerr's solution, albeit a complicated one, was to translate the motion from the horizontal to the vertical plane, thereby increasing the number of pin joints from nine to 14. In 1917 St Rollox had outlined an outside-cylindered version of Pickersgill's standard 4-4-0 utilising '60' class cylinders. The proposal was taken a stage further in 1918 with the provision of outside Walschaerts valve gear operating long lap (1½in)/long travel (6in) piston valves. This 4-4-0 was never built, but this lap and travel was specified for the new three-cylinder 4-6-0s.

Newly run-in No 956 underwent indicator trials between Carlisle and Glasgow and Perth during August 1921. Only one unspecified cylinder was indicated and this developed a maximum recorded IHP of 445 at a cut-off of 27 per cent at a speed of 57mph, up a rising gradient of 1 in 528. By this time all four engines had entered traffic and within six months drawings had been produced for the substitution of a set of Stephenson link motion to operate the inside piston valve, despite the fact Walschaerts gear operated the outside valves.

In 1978 the writer was fortunate to discuss the complicated question of the '956' valve gear with Mr G. R. M. Miller, who had started at St Rollox in 1911 as an apprentice of J. F. McIntosh, whom he recalled with great affection. Graeme Miller eventually retired in 1958 after 20 years as Chief Draughtsman there. He maintained that the failure of the derived valve gear was not that its steam distribution was poor, it was actually quite good, but that its high reciprocating mass resulted in abnormal wear and tear.

It has been stated that the two Carlisle engines, Nos 957 and 958, were rebuilt with Stephenson valve gear in April 1922, but there is photographic evidence that No 956 was also so modified. (Conversely, the writer has yet to find a photograph of Nos 957-8 when new showing the vertical rocking levers which took the motion from the outside valve spindles.) The indirect Stephenson valve gear proved unsatisfactory in another respect, in that the eccentric rods were crossed thereby giving decreasing lead as the engine was notched up, causing sluggish performance.

Pickersgill was thereupon anxious to persevere with the derived motion, which was completely redesigned in December 1922. The reciprocating mass was reduced, principally by bringing forward the main pivot from 13½ft to 8¼ft behind the inside-cylinder centre, and by shortening the valve gear connecting rods from 5ft to 4ft. Graeme Miller was instructed to make for a Pickersgill a model of the new layout in hardboard, and the Chief duly satisfied, the improved arrangement was subsequently applied to Nos 956 and 959.

There were still problems with inertia forces for a further necessary modification was the provision of cushioning cylinders, or dashpots. Graeme Miller recalls that these emitted a whistle, whose pitch depended upon the size of the holes drilled in them, a haunting sound which he associates with the demise of the Caledonian Railway in 1923.

Valve Gear Development on the CR '956' class, 1919-1923

St Rollox

Drawing No	Date	Description	Notes
19968	21 May 1919	Derived valve motion for inside cylinder	Manual reverse, separate splashers
20179	2 Oct 1919	As above	As built (steam reverse, combined splashers)
21396	24 Dec 1921	Arrangement of inside Stephenson valve gear	Vertical rocking lever
22060	29 Dec 1922	Modified derived valve gear for inside cylinder	Reduced reciprocating weight
22376	Oct 1923	Arrangement of dashpots	

Few of the original tracings detailed above now exist, but fortunately for the benefit of posterity Graeme Miller had retained copy prints from which the data has been taken. Curiously, none of the drawings quote the cardinal valve factors of lap, lead and maximum travel, which nevertheless can be determined from the relative proportions of the combination lever, etc. Ironically the Caledonian '956' engines constituted the only locomotive class

inherited by the LMS to incorporate piston valves having long travel *and* long lap (ie in excess of 1¼in). Nevertheless the class was conspicuous by its absence from the various competitive locomotive trials held during 1923-6, during which the characteristics of the smaller two-cylinder '60' class were determined. Combining the latter with the data from the indicator trials with No 956 in 1921, one can estimate that in theory at least the three-cylinder engine could have peaked at around 1,050DBHP over the 40-50mph speed range. This would certainly have made it comparable with its English LMS counterparts in Power Class 5, the Crewe and Horwich four-cylinder 4-6-0s.

It is interesting to note that Derby prepared a diagram showing the '956' class superimposed upon the Midland Division loading gauge, upon which the former did not notably impinge, but Pickersgill's three-cylinder masterpiece never ventured south of Carlisle. By 1925 this small class was largely relegated to freight duties, running on average only 24,000 miles *per annum* (compared to 32,000 miles by the '60' class) prior to its premature retirement in the early 1930s. It has even been suggested that it inspired the Royal Scots, but the two classes had very little in common other than their divided three-cylinder drive and boiler diameter (5ft 9in), and the fact that they were both designed and built in Glasgow!

Below: Power Curves for LMS Power Class 4 4-6-0s on 350ton trains 1923-1926.

LNWR No 388 (indirect Joy motion), Leeds-Carlisle, 1923.— — —

LNWR No 90 (direct Joy motion), Preston-Carlisle, 1925. ·········

(CR) LMS No 14630, Preston-Carlisle, 1926. ———

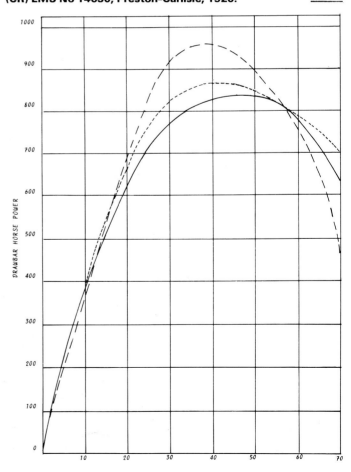

Proposed McIntosh 4-6-2 Locomotives, October 1913

	Narrow firebox	Wide firebox
Date	2 Oct 1913	8 Oct 1913
Cylinders (4)	16in × 26in	16in × 26in
Driving wheel dia	6ft 6in	6ft 6in
Boiler Pressure	180lb	180lb
Max Boiler dia	5ft 8in	5ft 8in
Tube length	20ft 6in	22ft 0in
Tube H.S.	2,456sq ft	2,440sq ft
Firebox	172sq ft	158sq ft
Evaporative	2,628sq ft	2,598sq ft
Superheater	516sq ft	516sq ft
Grate Area	27.0sq ft	37.0sq ft
Adhesive Weight (tons)	55.0	55.0
Locomotive weight (tons)	90.0	90.0
Tractive Effort	24,600lb	24,600lb

Below: The Caledonian Railway extensively photographed its first two 4-6-0s, Nos 49 and 50, completed at St Rollox early in 1903. Both were rebuilt with superheaters and piston valves in 1911, and subsequently with new frames and cylinders c1923. Both engines were scrapped by the LMS in 1933, 30 years after this posed photograph of No 49 at the head of some LNWR stock was taken near St Rollox
Courtesy, National Railway Museum, York

Bottom: In 1917 *Cardean* came off the regular 'Corridor' workings between Glasgow and Carlisle, being superseded by a Pickersgill '60' class 4-6-0. Here No 63 in pristine condition heads the 'Up Corridor' near Rockcliffe. *Real Photographs*

Above: One of the last surviving Pickersgill '60' class 4-6-0s, of the LMS-built 1925-6 series, as BR No 54640, heads a passenger train near Balornock in September 1952. *C. Lawson Kerr*

Below: An impressive rear three-quarter study of the prototype Pickersgill three-cylinder 4-6-0 No 956. This photograph was taken during the short period when the engine was provided with inside Stephenson valve gear, before being re-fitted with a modified form of derived valve gear.

Bottom: '956' class 4-6-0, LMS No 14801, hauling a freight train tender first.

Right: The CR '49' class were not an unqualified success and from them were developed the five '903' class engines of 1906. Here No 903 itself, the legendary *Cardean* stands in Platform 2 at Glasgow Central, awaiting departure with the 2pm up 'Corridor Diner', its regular duty for 10 years.
Courtesy, National Railway Museum, York

Above left: One of the two McIntosh 6ft 6in passenger 4-6-0s of 1903, No 50 *Sir James Thompson* in original condition.
LGRP, courtesy David & Charles

The original Pickersgill 4–6–0 under three ownerships: **(Left)** In its prime in Caley blue as CR No 60 it hauls an express near Stirling c1921. **(Above)** In crimson lake as LMS No 14650 sporting a '903' pattern chimney c1925. **(This picture)** at the end of its days in unlined black as BR No 54650, Pickersgill's first 4–6–0 hauls a short train of empty wagons near Uddington in June 1952.
A. G. Ellis, E. R. Wethersett

Appendices

Appendix 1
LNWR 4-6-0 Stock 1903-22

Number in Service

	'1400'	19in	'Experiment'	'Prince'	'Claughton'	Total
1903	10					10
1904	20					20
1905	30		5			35
1906	30	5	35			70
1907	30	55	45			130
1908	30	145	45			220
1909	30	170	100			300
1910	30	170·	105			305
1911	30	170	105	10		315
1912	30	170	105	10		315
1913	29	170	105	26	10	330
1914	20	170	105	40	20	355
1915	15	170	105	50	20	360
1916	4	170	105	90	30	399
1917	4	170	105	90	60	429
1918	4	170	105	90	60	429
1919	2	170	105	144	60	481
1920	0	170	105	155	100	530
1921	0	170	105	216	130	621
1922*	0	170	105	245	130	650

* LNWR Division A only
Dates to period ending 31 December

Appendix 2

LNWR Locomotive Repair Costs, 1922

Class	No in Class	Average age at 31/12/22 yr.	mth.	Total repair cost	Average repair cost per engine	Relative repair cost non-super-heated 'Precursor' = 1.00
'Precursor'	82	17	1	£37.434	£455	1.00
'Superheated Precursor'	48	17	6	£44.166	£920	2.02
'George V'	90	10	10	£82,584	£918	2.02
'Experiment'	104	14	9	£68,011	£654	1.44
'Prince'	245	4	3	£122,224	£499	1.10
'Claughton'	130	4	3	£118,652	£913	2.00
19in 4-6-0	170	14	9	£99,932	£588	1.29
Prospero	1	15	3	£771	£771	1.70

Appendix 3

Hughes 4-6-0 No 10455 – A Case History

Authorised 16 August 1923 as a 4-6-4T. Completed at Horwich Works as a 4-6-0 tender locomotive in July 1924, to Lot 83, Works No 1364, cost £5,199. Renumbered BR No 50455, we 25 December 1948. Withdrawn from service, we 6 October 1951. Broken up we 16 February 1952.

Shed Allocations

Carlisle Upperby	new
Newton Heath	5 November 1932
Farnley Junction	31 December 1932
Newton Heath	20 April 1935
Blackpool	21 September 1935 until withdrawal

Boilers Fitted (from 1 January 1927)

February 1928		ex-No 10469 (4-6-0)
20 April 1929		ex-No 10408 (4-6-0)
24 June 1930		ex-No 10461 (4-6-0)
23 August 1933		ex-No 11117 (4-6-4T)
11 March 1936		ex-No 10457 (4-6-0)
17 June 1938	No 4780	ex-No 11118 (4-6-4T)
23 April 1943	No 4779	ex-No 11118 (4-6-4T)
24 December 1948	No 5245	ex-No 11116 (4-6-4T)

Tenders Fitted (from 1 January 1927)

LYR	No 1694	new
LYR	No 1703	from 31 December 1932
LYR	No 1713	from 27 July 1944

Below: No 5671 *Arethusa* at Willesden on an up stopping train, November 1931. *E. R. Wethersett*

Annual Mileages

	Annual mileage	Coal issued tons*	Coal lb/mile*
1926	58,284†	—	—
1927	31,299	710	50.8
1928	31,262	809	58
1929	35,035	869	55.5
1930	38,996	914	52.5
1931	26,691	750	63
1932	17,754	506	64
1933	18,267	499	61
1934	31,902	842	59
1935	28,392	779	61
1936	38,495	1004	58
1937	35,291	936	59
1938	35,205	887	56
1939	38,868		
1940	35,539		
1941	34,602		
1942	23,923		
1943	26,126		
1944	26,923		
1945	27,940		
1946	23,754		
1947	20,208		
1948	15,499		
1949	20,569		
1950	22,953		
1951	6,869		
Total	751,208		

* Not recorded after 1938.
† From new.
Date to period ending 31 December.

Western Division	19in	'Expt'	'Prince'	'Claughton'	Class 8	Total
21 September 1932						
Camden			6	11 + 5*		22
Willesden			11			11
Bletchley	3	4	3			10
Nuneaton	5	6				11
Northampton			2	2		4
Bescot		4				4
Rugby	3	2	9	3		17
Walsall		3	3			6
Aston		3	2			5
Monument Lane			7			7
Bushbury	8	2			10	
Stafford	7		7			14
Crewe	17		48	38		105
Longsight	9		15	4 + 1*		29
Stockport	5		1			6
Birkenhead	14	2	2			18
Chester	1			3 + 4*		8
Bangor	4	1		3		8
Holyhead	6		7			13
Warrington		8				8
Sutton Oak		2				2
Springs Branch	13		13			26
Edge Hill	10		13	3 + 5*		31
Preston	3		11	2 + 5*		21
Carlisle (Upperby)	3		7		20	30
Shrewsbury	1		8			9
Abergavenny	3		3			6
Workington			2			2
Swansea	6					6
Patricroft	6		24	3		33
Carnforth	3		6			9
Mold Junction	3					3
Llandudno Junction	2	2	6	5		15
Barrow	3		3			6
Stoke		4	2			6
Total	138	43	221	77 + 20*	20	519

* Claughton rebuilt with G9½S boiler, those with Caprotti valve gear were equally divided between Camden and Edge Hill.
Three-cylinder conversions are not shown.

Appendix 4

Distribution of ex-LNWR and LYR 4-6-0s 1932-33

Central Division	19in	'Expt'	'Prince'	Claughton'	Class 8	Total
1 October 1932						
Newton Heath			5		8	13
Low Moor			3		4	7
Farnley Junction	11		10			21
Wakefield					1	1
Hillhouse	7	2				9
Agecroft					3	3
Lees (Oldham)	3					3
Southport					7	7
Bank Hall					5	5
Blackpool Central					22	22
Total	21	2	18		50	91

Midland Division						
September 1933						
Leeds				5		5
Carlisle (Durran Hill)				3		3
Total				8		8

Appendix 5

Summary of West Coast 4-6-0s

LNWR Class	Pre-1923 Nos	Built	LMS Nos	Withdrawn
'1400'	Between 170 and 2339	1903-1905	—	1913-1920
'Experiment'	Between 61 and 2646	1905-1910	5450-5554	1925-1935
'Prince'	Between 17 and 2520	1911-1922 (1924)	5600-5845	1933-1949
'Claughton'	Between 6 and 2511	1913-1921	5900-6029	1929-1949
19in	Between 3 and 2656	1906-1909	8700-8869	1931-1950
LYR				
'8'	1506-1525	1908-1909	10400-10404*	1925-1926
			10405-10419	1933-1949
	1649-(1683)	1921-1923	10420-10454	1934-1949
	—	1924-1925	10455-10474	1935-1951
CR				
'49'	49-50	1903	14750-14751	1933
'903'	903-907	1906	14752-14755	(1915)-1930
'60'	60-65	1916-1917	14650-14655	1944-1953
	—	1925-1926	14630-14649	1948-1953
'956'	956-959	1921	14800-14803	1931-1935

* Conversions, 1920-1921.

Tables of leading dimensions

Table A · **Leading dimensions of LNWR inside-cylinder 4-6-0 classes***

	'19in'	'Experiment'	'Prince'	'Modernised Prince' (proposed)
Cylinders	(I) 19in × 26in	(I) 19in × 26in	(I) 20½in × 26in	(I) 19½in × 26in
Driving Wheel dia	5ft 2½in	6ft 3in	6ft 3in	6ft 3in
Boiler pressure (lb)	175 & 180	175 & 180	175 & 180	200
Tube length	12ft 10½in/12ft 8⅝in	13ft 0in/12ft 10in	13ft 0in/12ft 10in	12ft 10in
Tube HS (sq ft)	1,765/1,674	1,781/1,688	1,376/1,308	1,308
Firebox (sq ft)	144/151	133/140	136/140	140
Total evaporative (sq ft)	1,909/1,825	1,914/1,824	1,512/1,448	1,448
Superheater (sq ft)	–/–	–/–	304/304	304
Grate area (sq ft)	25.0/26.0	25.0/26.0	25.0/26.0	26.0
Adhesion Weight (tons)	44.2	46.7	46.75	47.3
Engine weight (tons)	63.0	65.75	66.25	67.0
Coupled wheelbase	13ft 7in	13ft 7in	13ft 7in	13ft 7in
Engine wheelbase	26ft 8½in	26ft 8½in	26ft 8½in	27ft 5½in
Tender weight (tons)	37.0	37.0	39.25	42.7
Coal capacity (tons)	6	6	6	5½
Water capacity (gal)	3,000	3,000	3,000	3,500
Overall length	57ft 9in	57ft 9in	57ft 9in	58ft 11¼in
Tractive effort (lb)	22,400	19,500	21,700	22,400

* Boiler dimensions are shown thus: Round Topped/Belpaire.
(I) inside cylinders.

TABLE B · **Leading dimensions of LNWR four-cylinder 4-6-0 classes and rebuilds**

	'1400'	Prospero	'Claughton' 1913/1920	Reboilered 'Claughton'	3-Cylinder 5X Rebuild 1930/1932-4
Cylinders	2HP 15in × 24in 2LP 20½in × 24in	(4) 14in × 26in	(4) 16/15¾in × 26in	(4) 15¾in × 26in	(3) 18in × 26in
Driving wheel dia	5ft 2½in	6ft 3in	6ft 9in	6ft 9in	6ft 9in
Boiler pressure (lb)	200	175	175	200	200
Boiler diameter	4ft 8in	5ft 2in	5ft 2in	5ft 5⅛in	5ft 5⅛in
Tube length	13ft 4in	13ft 0in	14ft 10½in	14ft 0in	14ft 0in
Tube HS (sq ft)	1,564	1,376	1,647/1,574	1,550	1,550/1,450
Firebox (sq ft)	123	136	171/175	183	183/183
Total evaporative (sq ft)	1,687	1,512	1,818/1,749	1,733	1,733/1,633
Superheater (sq ft)	—	304	414/379	365	365/365
Grate area (sq ft)	20.6	25.0	30.5	30.5	30.5
Adhesion weight (tons)	44.0	Not recorded	59.0	59.4	59.75/59.75
Engine weight (tons)	60.0	Not recorded	77.75	79.0	80.75/80.75
Coupled wheelbase	11ft 6in	13ft 7in	15ft 3in	15ft 3in	15ft 3in/15ft 4in
Engine wheelbase	24ft 6in	26ft 8in	29ft 0in	29ft 0in	27ft 5½in/27ft 5½in
Tender weight (tons)	31.6	37.0	39.25	40.75	42.7
Coal capacity (tons)	5	6	6	6	5½
Water capacity (gal)	2,500	3,000	3,000	3,000	3,500
Overall length	56ft 10½in	57ft 9in	63ft 4¾in	63ft 4¾in	62ft 8¾in
Tractive effort (lb)	26,300	20,300	24,500/23,700	27,100	26,500

TABLE C **Leading dimensions of LYR Hughes 4-6-0 and 4-6-4T**

	Nos 1506-1525 as built	*Conversions 1920-1921*	*Nos 10455 -10474*	*4-6-4T*
Cylinders	(4) 16in × 26in	(4) $16\frac{1}{2}$in × 26in	(4) $16\frac{1}{2}$in × 26in	(4) $16\frac{1}{2}$in × 26in
Driving wheel dia	6ft 3in	6ft 3in	6ft 3in	6ft 3in
Boiler pressure (lb)	180	180	180	180
Tube length	15ft 0in	14ft 8in	14ft 8in	14ft 8in
Tube HS (sq ft)*	2,317	1,511	1,729	1,729
Firebox (sq ft)*	190	175	180	180
Total evaporation (sq ft)*	2,507	1,686	1,909	1,909
Superheater (sq ft)*	—	552	504	504
Grate area (sq ft)	27.0	27.0	29.6	29.6
Adhesion weight (tons)	59.0	59.3	59.7	56.5
Engine weight (tons)	77.1	79.05	77.45	99.95
Coupled wheelbase	13ft 7in	13ft 7in	13ft 7in	13ft 7in
Engine wheelbase	25ft 4in	25ft 7in	26ft 7in	40ft 4in
Tender weight (tons)	30.65	31.15	40.0	
Coal capacity (tons)	5	5	6	$3\frac{1}{2}$
Water capacity (gal)	2,480	2,480	3,000	2,000
Overall length	57ft $5\frac{3}{4}$in	57ft $8\frac{3}{4}$in	61ft $4\frac{3}{4}$in	49ft $10\frac{1}{2}$in
Tractive effort (lb)	27,200	28,800	28,800	28,800

* Horwich practice prior to 1923 was to calculate heating surface on the fireside, thus reducing evaporative and increasing superheater surface.

TABLE D **Leading dimensions of CR superheated 4-6-0 passenger classes**

	'49'	*'903'*	*Proposed O/C 4-6-0*	*'60'*	*'956'*
Cylinders	(I) $20\frac{3}{4}$in × 26in	(I) $20\frac{3}{4}$in × 26in	(0) 21in × 26in	(0) 20in × 26in	(3) $18\frac{1}{2}$in × 26in
Driving wheel dia	6ft 6in	6ft 6in	6ft 6in	6ft 1in	6ft 1in
Boiler pressure (lb)	175	175	170	175	180
Boiler diameter	5ft 0in	5ft $3\frac{1}{2}$in	5ft $3\frac{1}{2}$in	5ft $3\frac{1}{2}$in	5ft 9in
Tube length	15ft 8in	16ft 8in	c15ft 8in	15ft 3in	16ft 0in
Tube HS (sq ft)	1,509	1,666	1,578	1,529	2,200
Firebox (sq ft)	145	148	148	147	170
Total evaporative (sq ft)	1,654	1,814	1,726	1,676	2,370
Superheater (sq ft)	516	516	487	258	270
Grate Area (sq ft)	26.0	26.0	26.0	25.5	28.0
Adhesion weight (tons)	54.5	55.75	54.25E	56.5	60.0
Engine weight (tons)	71.5	74.25	73.75E	75.0	81.0
Coupled wheelbase	15ft 0in	14ft 8in	14ft 8in	14ft 6in	15ft 0in
Engine wheelbase	28ft 8in	28ft 8in	27ft 4in	27ft 6in	28ft 8in
Tender weight (tons)	55.0	57.0	56.0	46.5	48.0
Coal capacity (tons)	5	5	6	6	$5\frac{1}{2}$
Water capacity (gal)	5,000	5,000	4,600	4,200	4,500
Overall length	65ft 6in	65ft 6in	64ft 9in	62ft 6in	63ft 8in
Tractive effort (lb)	21,300	21,300	21,300	21,200	28,000

E = Estimated. (I) = Inside cylinders. (O) = Outside cylinders

TABLE E **Valve characteristics of West Coast multi-cylinder 4-6-0 classes**

Railway/class	*LNWR*	*'1400'*	*LNWR Prospero*	*LNWR 'Claughton'*	*LYR Class 8**	*CR '956'*
Cylinders	HP (2) 15in × 24in	LP (2) $20\frac{1}{2}$in × 24in	(4) 14in × 26in	(4) $15\frac{3}{4}$in × 26in	(4) $16\frac{1}{2}$in × 26in	(3) $18\frac{1}{2}$in × 26in
Valves	$6\frac{1}{2}$in PV	slide	12in PV	8in PV	9in PV	8in PV
Lap	$\frac{7}{8}$in	$\frac{13}{16}$in	$\frac{7}{8}$in	1in	$1\frac{3}{16}$in	$1\frac{1}{2}$in
Lead	$\frac{3}{16}$in	$\frac{1}{2}$in	$\frac{1}{8}$in	$\frac{5}{32}$in	$\frac{1}{4}$in	$\frac{1}{4}$in
Exhaust clearance	$\frac{3}{16}$in	$\frac{1}{16}$in	nil	$\frac{1}{16}$in	nil	nil
Maximum travel in full gear	$4\frac{1}{8}$in	$5\frac{1}{8}$in	$4\frac{1}{4}$in	$4\frac{9}{32}$in	$6\frac{3}{8}$in	6in
Valve gear type	Joy	Joy	Dendy Marshall	Walschaerts	Walschaerts	Walschaerts /Pickersgill

PV = piston valve

* Superheated, details for original non-superheated slide valve engines not known, lap was increased to $1\frac{7}{16}$in in the last 20 engines.

Bibliography

North Western Steam, by W. A. Tuplin, George Allen & Unwin 1963.

The LNWR Precursor Family, by O. S. Nock, David & Charles 1966.

The Claughton and Baby Scot Classes, compiled and published by E. E. Robinson, 1934.

The British Locomotive Catalogue 1825-1923, Volume 2B, by B. & D. Baxter, Moorland Pub Co 1979.

The Lancashire & Yorkshire Railway in the Twentieth Century, by Eric Mason, Ian Allan Ltd 1954.

Forty Years of Caledonian Locomotives 1882-1922, by H. J. Campbell Cornwall, David & Charles 1974.

The Scottish 4-6-0 Classes, by C. P. Atkins, Ian Allan Ltd 1976.

Locomotive Panorama, Vol 1, by E. S. Cox, Ian Allan Ltd 1965.

Chronicles of Steam, by E. S. Cox, Ian Allan Ltd 1967.

Speaking of Steam, by E. S. Cox, Ian Allan Ltd 1971.

Periodicals consulted:
The Engineer
Engineering
Journal of the Institution of Locomotive Engineers
Journal of the Stephenson Locomotive Society
The Locomotive Magazine
Locomotive News & Railway Notes
Proceedings of the Institution of Civil Engineers
Proceedings of the Institution of Mechanical Engineers
The Railway Engineer
The Railway Gazette
The Railway Magazine
The Railway Observer
Railway World
Trains Illustrated

Published drawings

London & North Western Railway
'1400' class, Not published.
'Experiment', *The Engineer*, 6 October 1905.
19in Goods, *Locomotive Magazine*, May 1907.
'Prince', Not published.
'Claughton', *The Engineer*, 6 June 1913. *The Railway Engineer*, June 1913. *The Railway Gazette*, 6 June 1917.

Lancashire & Yorkshire Railway
Original 4-6-0, *Engineering*, 30 July 1909.
Superheated 4-6-0, Not published, but the corresponding 4-6-4T was described in *The Railway Engineer* for June 1924.

Caledonian Railway
'49/50 class, Not published.
'903' class, *Engineering*, 1 February 1907.
'60' class, *The Engineer*, 4 November 1921.
'956' class, *The Railway Engineer*, October 1921.

Below: One of the original 1911 batch of 'Princes', No 1691 *Pathfinder*, **since repainted in unlined black livery, at Shap with a down express.** *Rixon Bucknall Collection*

Index